STO

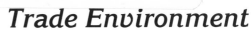

*Trade Environment*

## DO NOT REMOVE
## CARDS FROM POCKET

# The Changing Hemispheric Trade Environment: Opportunities and Obstacles

*Mark B. Rosenberg, Editor*

**Florida International University**
Latin American and Caribbean Center

**White & Case**

Miami, Florida • 1991

Latin American and Caribbean Center, Florida International University, University Park, Miami, Florida 33199

Library of Congress Cataloging-in-Publication Data

The Changing hemispheric trade environment : opportunites and
    obstacles / Mark B. Rosenberg, editor.
        p.  cm.
    Includes bibliographical references.
    ISBN 1-879862-01-8 (pbk.) : $11.95
    1. Latin America—Commercial policy. 2. Latin America—Commerce—
Europe. 3. Europe—Commerce—Latin America. 4. Latin America—
Commerce—Japan. 5. Japan—Commerce—Latin America. 6. America—
Commercial policy.  I. Rosenberg, Mark B.
HF 1480.5.C454  1991
382'.098—dc20                                                      91-32431
                                                                        CIP

*Not printed at state expense.*
*Printed on recycled paper.*

# Contents

v

# Preface

President George Bush's Enterprise for the Americas Initiative and the coincident national debate on a free trade agreement with Mexico reflect the growing importance of trade issues in foreign and domestic affairs. Nations throughout the world are restructuring their trade relations, seeking to ensure access to international markets and capital.

The 1990s will witness the emergence of a single European market, the initial economic evolution of the former communist bloc countries, and the expansion of the influence of Asian countries, most notably Japan, in Latin America. The decade may also mark the emergence of a unified North American free trade area. These and other trade developments are destined to change trade relations in the Western Hemisphere. Despite the extensive news coverage devoted to these developments, there has been limited discourse on the impact they will have on the patterns of trade.

*The Changing Hemispheric Trade Environment: Opportunities and Obstacles* is a product of a partnership between White & Case and the Latin American and Caribbean Center (LACC) of Florida International University. The purpose of the partnership is to raise the level of public and scholarly awareness about the opportunities and obstacles to enhance trade in the hemisphere. This book is a collection of commissioned and revised studies initially presented in Miami, Florida, on January 10, 1991, at a conference sponsored by LACC and White & Case. It examines the multidimensional and multiregional nature of the current trade environment. The contributors not only analyze the trade options and possible configurations of hemispheric trade partnerships and the likely trade impact of the single European market. They also explore developments that are commonly neglected in the current debate over hemispheric

vii

trade, namely, the possible roles of Japan and the Uruguay Round of the General Agreement on Tariffs and Trade.

*The Changing Hemispheric Trade Environment* is a valuable contribution to the national debate on trade issues, and will stand as a lasting contribution to the scholarly literature on international trade.

James B. Hurlock
Chairman, Management Committee
White & Case
New York, New York
May 1991

# Acknowledgements

The law firm of White & Case and the Latin American and Caribbean Center (LACC) of Florida International University conducted a one-day conference on "The Changing Hemispheric Trade Environment in Latin America" on January 10, 1991. This gathering brought together trade specialists, representatives from the private sector, and scholars to examine the major developments that will structure hemispheric trade relations in the 1990s.

From the commissioned papers and the commentaries, we have assembled a book that will help to answer many of the key questions that are now emerging about the future of hemispheric trade relations.

This book would not have been possible without the efforts and interest of Larry Gragg and Tony Alvarez of White & Case. In LACC, Melanie Smalley, Douglas Kincaid, Richard Tardanico, Teresita Marill, Raquel Jurado, and Michelle Acebo provided invaluable assistance in all the aspects of conference design and coordination. We owe special thanks to Sofía López and René Ramos in LACC who have pooled their skills and talents to edit and produce this book.

# Introduction: The Changing Hemispheric Trade Environment

## Mark B. Rosenberg

Following a decade of lost economic opportunities in Latin America as a result of the debt crisis and intense Great Power competition, there is a new surge of optimism, hope, and uncertainty throughout the hemisphere. Critical issues, such as democracy, environmental protection, and the development of more effective justice systems, continue to grow in importance. As a result, the agenda of inter-American concerns is being transformed.[1]

Among the major factors accounting for this transformation are the decline of hostilities between the United States and the Soviet Union and the movement toward a Single European Market (SEM) in 1992. Despite President George Bush's efforts to promote a "new world order" in the post-Persian Gulf era, there are no guarantees that anticommunism as a policy will be replaced by a clear set of new directions in US foreign policy. Anticommunism in the United States has been not only a policy but a basic value of life. As a result, the issues emerging in the wake of anticommunism are a "mixed bag of incomplete and sometimes incompatible ideas."[2]

Nowhere is this "mixed bag" clearer than in the area of trade policy. As Henry Nau comments, "international trade is mostly a matter of domestic politics . . ." and "the future of the trading system depends on the domestic choices" that industrial and developing countries will make over the next few years.[3] In the post-Cold War era, escalating conflict in the trade arena will clearly demonstrate the inherent contradictions of competing interests in public policy during the 1990s.

Thus, the trade terrain will be a singularly important arena for world conflict during the 1990s. In the Western Hemisphere, a range of new forces and developments presents unprecedented challenges and op-

1

portunities, and will dramatically alter the nature of hemispheric trade relations:

- The likely emergence of regional and subregional trade arrangements, including the Enterprise for the Americas Initiative (EAI), the North American Free Trade Agreement, and the SEM in 1992.
- The growing importance of Japan for world trade and finance and its potential role in altering hemispheric trade patterns.
- The Uruguay Round of the General Agreement on Tariffs and Trade (GATT).

## The Emerging Trade Environment

After nearly a decade of economic experimentation, there seems to be a general consensus throughout Latin America and the Caribbean that structural adjustment and free markets offer potent alternatives to previous economic development efforts. In this view, international trade and development of the external sector are key elements of renewed economic growth.

President Bush's proposal to create a hemispheric free trade zone with the EAI opens the door to serious discussions throughout Latin America and the Caribbean about the region's destiny. The Bush plan, based upon a call for open markets, new debt measures, and support for investment, offers an unprecedented opportunity for the region to gain secure access to the US market and to new investment capital.[4]

On the heels of the agreement between the United States and Mexico to initiate negotiations for a free trade agreement, the Bush plan has been motivated by a genuine US concern for the specter of global trading blocs and the possible exclusion of the United States. As Gary Hufbauer and Jeffrey Schott suggest in the following chapter, the response from Latin America and the Caribbean has been positive. Assertive leadership is now moving the thirteen countries of the Caribbean toward a single regional market and economy by 1993.[5] Andean countries are reexamining their regional trade arrangements and have set forth a bold new effort to reduce trade barriers. Southern Cone countries have concrete plans to open their borders to products from their respective neighbors. Central America has taken some steps to invigorate regional trade, but civil turmoil there and the absence of strong leadership continue to hamper collective state action.

Most dramatically, Mexico has moved rapidly to end its traditional diplomatic and commercial isolation.[6] In response to Latin American concerns about the potential trade and investment diversion impact of privileged access for Mexico to the US market, Mexico has mounted an aggressive campaign to cooperate with Caribbean and Central and South American neighbors.

Flexibility is the hallmark of the EAI's trade dimension. At this point, there are more questions than answers. Will the prospect of free trade with the United States promote bilateralism in the region or will it foster regional cohesiveness among groups of countries with similar levels of resource endowments? Will free trade with the United States reduce intraregional trade and how will it affect the understandings fostered through GATT? How will countries maximize their bargaining leverage with the United States in trade negotiations?

If Latin America and the Caribbean are to protect their interests, they will need to develop an expanded base of knowledge about the changing global economy, including new methods of production and the restructuring of international trade. Since the United States and Canada will offer a huge new market, there will need to be greater awareness about these markets and their consumer preferences. Finally, a potentially frenzied rush to restructure local economies cannot come at the cost of diminished rights and protection for labor and the working class in Latin America. Inevitably, great tension will result between the economic demands of free trade and the pressure to reduce rather than expand political freedom.

The case of Mexico is important because it will be Latin America's first country to negotiate a free trade agreement with the United States. The Mexican experience will provide important lessons for trade negotiators throughout the region.

## The United States and Mexico

Following years of mutual hostilities and tensions, there is a new tone to US-Mexican relations as both countries attempt to sort out their trade interests. The primary ingredient for this new phase of harmony has been the political will of the leadership of both countries. President Carlos Salinas de Gortari has willingly tempered the most strident anti-US aspects of Mexican nationalism to seek a new high ground in bilateral relations. Moreover, he has led a process of restructuring the

Mexican economy that has had high short-term costs, especially for Mexican labor.[7] A critical factor to this process has been the growing receptivity to reform of key segments of the country's private sector, traditionally one of the most protected and privileged in the Western Hemisphere.

In the United States, President Bush has continually demonstrated his interest in improving relations with Mexico and is firmly committed to the deepening of trade relations with that country. The Bush administration, however, has underestimated the political potency of the forces unleashed against the pact with Mexico. An alliance—including environmentalists, human rights promoters, labor unions, and Mexicophobes—is ganging up to stop the US-Mexico proposal.[8]

Free trade negotiations will focus on major agenda items as Hufbauer and Schott point out, including tariff and quota issues, agriculture, energy, the automobile industry, services, the *maquiladora*, and countervailing duty and antidumping issues.

Assessments of risks and benefits to both parties are numerous. In the United States, the primary advantage to free trade is the opening of the Mexican market and the investment possibilities there.[9] For the Mexican private sector, predictable and stable access to the US market is a powerful rationale. But even more compelling is the access to new sources of finance in the context of the country's capital shortage. After eight years of capital flight, heavy debt, devaluation, and reduced productivity, new investment capital is in short supply.

Nonetheless, Mexicans also understand that an open trade system will not only alter the structure of trade and finance. It will likely accelerate the transition from family-owned companies to those with diversified shareholder ownership and professional management. For small and medium-sized businesses that do not have access to capital markets, the transition may be more abrupt unless they can find joint venture partners to infuse new levels of capital and technology. It is important to note, however, that the emerging free trade relationship between the United States and Mexico will have an array of costs and benefits that will vary across the production spectrum.

## The United States and Canada

The US-Canada free trade agreement will offer important lessons and guideposts for Mexico and other Latin American countries. One assessment of the agreement suggests that its impact has been mixed—perhaps more positive for the United States than for Canada. For instance, the Canadian Labor Congress states that thirty-six companies have closed facilities in Canada since the US-Canada free trade agreement was signed. A total of 11,064 jobs have been lost as a result. US firms are apparently using the liberalized foreign investment code to transform the companies into subsidiaries of existing Canadian-owned firms. In the process, little new productive capacity has been created in Canada.[10] Canadian and US industrialists, however, have requested accelerated tariff phase-outs for more than four hundred products that account for about $6 billion in bilateral trade. Subsidies still are to be negotiated.[11]

Canada's economy is far more advanced than Mexico's; there are major structural differences between the two countries. Thus, while lessons can be learned from the Canadian-US negotiations, they have their limits.

As Hufbauer and Schott suggest in chapter one, Canada's interest in joining the pending US-Mexico talks is defensive. In fact, it may be motivated to avoid a "hub-and-spoke" model of hemispheric trade. In such a scenario, the US hub would have a separate arrangement for each participating country or group of countries. Canada would risk losing Mexican trade to US-based companies. It could also lose investment to the United States because only US-based companies would enjoy tariff-free access to all three markets.[12]

Although there is optimism in both the United States and Mexico about the forthcoming negotiations, there are many obstacles to successful discussions. In the United States, President Bush may not have the political capital to fight protectionist interests throughout the country who will point to the large wage differentials between Mexican and US labor and who are focusing on other issues such as the environment as a means to slow down talks.[13] Those favorable to free trade in the private sector may not have the leadership and cohesion necessary to mount a successful campaign to support the president. Congress's tendency to micromanage foreign affairs and its appetite for Mexico-bashing could reverse the current era of goodwill between the two countries. In Mexico, continuing problems with that country's political opening and mounting evidence of widespread human rights abuses could undermine the government's capacity to continue its progress in structural adjustment—a key element underlying its free trade interests.

Mexico's involvement in a new North American trade arrangement has caused concern within Central America and the Caribbean. Leaders from both regions have publicly suggested that any US-Mexico agreement would be a major step in eroding preferential market access provided by the Caribbean Basin Initiative (CBI), which allows twenty-eight countries to ship a range of products duty free to the United States.[14] The general argument is that trade diversion would be possible because of Mexico's many advantages, including lower production costs, proximity to the US market and therefore cheaper transportation and communication costs, abundant natural resources, and a large domestic market.[15]

Versions abound concerning the impact of a US-Mexico agreement. Hufbauer and Schott's chapter suggests that the elimination of US tariffs on Mexican products will increase Mexican exports to the United States by about $1.4 billion in the short run. The elimination of both tariff and non-tariff barriers will increase Mexican exports by about $2.8 billion. The trade diversion impact on Central and South America is estimated at about $250 million over a five-year period. This figure, however, could rise if sector-specific arrangements on non-tariff barriers come at the expense of third countries.

Mexico and the countries of Central America have taken some steps to reorganize their trade relations in preparation for an eventual US-Mexico agreement. At a January 1991 meeting in Tuxtla Gutiérrez, a framework agreement was signed that calls for sectoral agreements leading to free trade in a range of products that will expand over the next six years.[16] In the context of this agreement, Mexico emerges as an intermediary, developing its own role as a "hub" with numerous other spokes—Central America, Venezuela and Colombia, and, at some point in the future, the Caribbean.

In practice, the Mexico-Central America agreement has only symbolic importance at this time. In relative terms, Central American exports to Mexico were only 0.2 percent of Mexico's total imports and Mexican exports to Central America totaled about 1.5 percent of total Mexican exports. Guatemala is Mexico's leading trade partner, with a total trade exceeding $130 million in 1987.[17]

Early concerns expressed about this agreement include fears that Central America's import and export costs will rise, since those countries will not be trading directly with the United States, and that the renewed Central American integration efforts will be put at risk.[18]

Riordan Roett's chapter warns against the cautiously optimistic approach taken by Hufbauer and Schott. He suggests that the real impediments to the enhancement of hemispheric trade are the continuing economic debt and the lack of capital and foreign direct investment. In the case of Mexico, he concludes, the major impediment is the continuing violation of human rights in that country.

## The New Europe and Latin America[19]

The fast-paced changes in Eastern Europe during 1989 and the pending unification of the Western European market in 1992 give Europe a new and central role in the emerging global economy. Transformation of the Soviet economy into a free-market system will give added weight to Europe's emerging leadership role.

For the foreseeable future, it is clear that Europe will be preoccupied with Europe, particularly in economic, trade, and political considerations. In general, as Wolf Grabendorff points out in his chapter, "asymmetry" tends to characterize Latin American trade with the European Community (EC). First, unlike other areas of the developing world, Latin America does not benefit from specific EC policies of preferences except for the General System of Preferences, which applies to all developing countries. Second, about three-quarters of Latin American exports to the EC are primary products, for which a relatively lower demand elasticity exists. Finally, there is a lack of diversification of Latin American exports to the EC, especially with regard to semimanufactured or manufactured goods.

What are some of the most recent trends in European-Latin American trade relations? The structure of trade between the EC and Latin America has a more typical North-South quality. Trade revolves around Latin American fuel, primary goods, and agricultural products in exchange for European industrial products. Indeed, Latin America has had a declining impact on European commercial markets during the last two decades, as Grabendorff's chapter suggests. In 1970, Latin America accounted for 8.1 percent of the imports and received 7.2 percent of the exports of the EC; in 1988, these figures dropped to 6.0 percent and 3.8 percent, respectively. More dramatically, in 1979, the EC had provided 27.3 percent of the imports and received 31.3 percent of the exports from Latin America. By 1988, these percentages had declined to 17.7 percent and 21.1 percent, respectively.

With some notable exceptions, Latin America has encountered increasing difficulty in exporting to the European market. As Henry Nau's chapter suggests, the EC's Common Agricultural Policy (CAP) has barred many Latin American agricultural products and prevented access to third markets because of highly competitive prices resulting from subsidies.

Although two Caribbean countries (Haiti and the Dominican Republic) have recently been given preferential access to the EC through the Lômé (IV) Convention, their entry carried explicit conditions to prohibit the entry of other low development countries. Central America was an obvious target of this restriction. One trade analyst has suggested that the purpose of the recent Lômé negotiations was to "prepare the Caribbean countries for life without preferences . . . as the EC seeks to globalize its relationship with the developing world and carve out its special trading relationship with Eastern Europe and the Mediterranean."[20]

Nevertheless, there are instances in several Latin American countries where the European presence is as important as the US presence and more significant than Japan's. What will be the impact of the SEM on these relations? Several general conclusions can be drawn:

- The initiation of the SEM will be accompanied by a new diversion of trade from other markets. While some traditional Latin American exports may be hurt, dramatic effects are not expected given the complementarity of the markets.
- The increase in European demand may offset the negative impact on traditional exports from the region, particularly in some product areas such as bananas.
- Pending the outcome of the Uruguay Round of GATT, a slow reduction in subsidies for agricultural production can be predicted.

In this context, the SEM's effects on commercial relations with Latin America are of less importance than with those regions of East Asia or traditional developed countries where manufactured goods dominate trade relations. The SEM's effects on Latin America, either positive or negative, are likely to be marginal since the SEM will have less impact on primary products than on manufactured goods.

Nonetheless, as Grabendorff points out, the SEM will have an impact on US-Latin American trade within a context of growing Latin American dependence on commercial relations with the United States. It is likely that the growing income effect brought about by the SEM in EC countries will affect positively aggregate import demand, including imports from the United States and Latin America. Thus, although Latin Americans had seen Europe as an important "third option," there is a new sense among many that the region is now marginal to European interests and concerns.

Eastern Europe's transition to open markets presents special challenges to Latin America and the Caribbean. Not counting the Soviet Union (with a population of 288 million people), the Eastern European market has some 137 million consumers. The economic conversion of these countries has clearly captured the interest of the industrial world, particularly Western European countries.

Eastern Europe has several distinct advantages for the foreign investor. First, it has both an industrial infrastructure and an industrial culture. Second, Eastern Europe's labor force is skilled and wages are low. Indeed, the average Eastern European worker makes about one-fifth or one-sixth the salary of a Western European counterpart. Third, geography and ethnicity favors intensified Western European interest in the new economies of the region. Finally, a number of Eastern European countries are adopting policies and legislation to encourage foreign investment. Privatization has been embraced and joint ventures are aggressively solicited. One observer has stated that "for the European investor, Eastern Europe today is like having his 'Asian NIC' of the future next door."[21]

Nonetheless, the early optimism about the region's rapid transition to market-based economies has been replaced by the sober recognition of the difficult process of transition. One analyst has stated that "while communism has been roundly defeated in Central Europe . . . its residual impact is hardly negligible. No magic wand can suddenly erase the habits and customs of four decades of communist rule . . . ."[22] In general, Eastern Europe's tendency to open markets can facilitate trade relations with Latin America. Latin America, however, has no specific advantage with the newly emerging market.

The fears of fortress Europe may well be exaggerated. In such a scenario, the trade loss to Latin America would not have a major impact on either partner. The specter of a giant European market, however, may function "to siphon foreign investment as a result of the productivity gains to be made by these [European] firms."[23]

## Japan's Role: Cooperation or Rivalry with the United States?

Japan's impressive economic development during the last two decades has led many Latin American leaders to consider a "Pacific Rim" strategy as a means to diversify trade and investment opportunities for their countries. Japan's potential importance for Latin America will become more apparent as the 1990s crystallize the co-equal status of Europe and Japan with the United States.

*Is Japan Interested in Latin America?* Although Latin America's attention toward Japan has grown in the 1980s, Japan's interests during the past decade have been focused elsewhere—on relations with the United States and with the booming Asian market. Japan views itself as being part of two triangles—one composed of Japan, the United States, and Europe, and the other of Japan, Asia Pacific, and the United States. While Japan's foreign assistance efforts now make it the largest aid donor in the world in absolute terms, its program tends to respond to pressure from other developed countries.[24]

As Barbara Stallings's chapter illustrates, Latin America's share of Japan's economic transactions has fallen, but the absolute value has been constant or increased slightly. Trade has tended to be the lagging sector in Japanese-Latin American relations. Japan's relations with the region are dominated by investment and financial concerns. It is estimated that Japan is now Latin America's leading creditor for medium and long-term private bank loans. Japanese banks hold about $46 billion of Latin American debt compared to about $36 billion held by US banks.

Total trade between Latin America and Japan amounted to $16.5 billion in 1989, about 3.6 percent of Japan's total trade. The high point in trade relations was in 1955, when Latin America accounted for about 9 percent of Japan's trade. Trade between Latin America and Japan tends to follow a traditional "colonial pattern." Raw materials are imported by Japan. Latin America receives industrial products.[25] Some key Latin American exports to Japan include iron ore, coffee, inwrought copper, ferroalloys, silver, pig iron, emeralds, forage, and salt. Stallings's chapter illustrates that Japan is more significant as an export market (10 percent of Latin American exports are sold there) than as a provider of imports (about 7 percent of imports originate in Japan.)

Brazil is Japan's largest Latin American trade partner after Panama.[26] With a surplus in its trade with Japan, Brazil accounted for 25 percent of

Japan's total Latin American trade in 1989, followed by Mexico (21%), Chile (11%), Colombia (4.5%), Venezuela (4.3%), Argentina (3.4%), Peru (3.3%), Ecuador (1.3%), and Honduras (1.1%).

In 1989, Japan was the second largest export market for Chile, Brazil, Peru, Honduras, and Mexico. Chile, in particular, has been able to increase its nontraditional product trade with Japan, especially in fish, fruits, and forestry products. Mexico's nonoil exports to Japan also increased by about 14 percent per annum in the late 1980s. For imports, Japan is the second largest source for Ecuador, Colombia, Panama, Honduras, Haiti, and Mexico.

Although Latin America has had success in trading raw materials and semimanufactured goods with Japan, the prospects for manufactured goods are not high. A major impediment is price competitiveness. As Tetsuro Iino's chapter suggests, the "tyranny of distance" plays against Latin American products as a result of longer shipping distances from most Latin American cities to Japan than to other major markets (i.e. in the United States). Other impediments include lower product quality, punctuality and stability of product delivery, aftercare service, and specialized consumer tastes.

As Stallings points out in her chapter, an important element in the evolving Japanese-Latin American trade relation is the role of Japanese trading companies, which have emerged as key trade promoters. They are involved in intermediating transactions, purchasing goods worldwide, and selling them in Japan (and increasingly to third countries). They act as bankers—financing trade and in some instances providing equity capital; and they gather and process information that is used for company decisionmaking. Six of the nine major Japanese trading companies have offices in thirteen or fourteen Latin American countries, including Cuba. Nine trading companies move about one-half of Japanese-Latin American trade and about 10 percent of all Latin American trade. The trading companies have been especially important for small and medium-sized firms in Japan and Latin America. These trading companies could be the major beneficiaries of enhanced trade in the Americas. During the 1980s, their third country efforts spiraled as Japanese domestic market demand for imports slowed.

*What Are the Implications for the United States?* Stallings suggests alternative scenarios for US-Latin American-Japanese trade relations in the 1990s: a Western Hemisphere trade bloc with an insignificant role for Japan, a Japanese "headquarters strategy" in which Japan replaces the United States, or a "cooperative" option in which the United States and Japan do not compete for market share in Latin America.

What appears likely at this point is the third scenario. As Stallings suggests, there is little interest in Japan for Latin America except for some special cases such as Mexico and Chile. Therefore, the United States will remain the main provider of opportunities for trade and investment in Latin America. The Japanese government will probably continue to show a willingness to help the United States, if for no other reason than because an improved trade balance with Latin America may take pressure off the Japanese.[27] But Latin American hopes that Japan can help in economic recovery and enhanced trade vigor are misplaced.

## The Uruguay Round

GATT is the principal multilateral body concerned with international trade. It comprises some one hundred member countries. GATT is credited with promoting a tenfold growth in the volume of international trade since World War II.

A new round of trade negotiations with fifteen groups initiated in 1986 was scheduled to end in December 1990. The intent was to further liberalize world trade and to go beyond GATT's traditional focus on tariffs. A major US objective in the discussions was to extend GATT coverage to new and previously unregulated areas of the global economy: agriculture, services,[28] and trade related to intellectual property and investment, which may account for up to one-third of the world's $4 trillion in trade. As a corollary, the hope for the Uruguay Round was to examine and regulate other types of trade barriers that have increased in importance as tariff barriers have diminished. Of particular US interest has been the elimination of agricultural subsidies that contribute to much of the estimated $94 million a year in the costs of agricultural protectionism on world trade.[29]

From the Latin American viewpoint, as the chapter by Luis Abugattas points out, the Round's importance revolves around two critical issues. First, a successful Round could provide a multilateral framework within which Latin America could protect itself from unilateral US impositions through the EAI. In the same vein, it could constitute a forum from which negotiations for privileged access to the US market for Latin America could be arranged in key sectors such as textiles, apparel, and tropical products. It would have also provided for measures to diminish non-tariff barriers to Latin American products.[30]

A second issue of importance for Latin America revolves around agriculture, where such exporting countries as Brazil, Argentina, Australia, and Canada, among others, united to form the Cairns Group. The objective of the group was reform of farm trade, particularly the EC's CAP. Stating that the reduction of farm subsidies would be a precondition for progress in such areas as trade in services and intellectual property, the developing countries, led by Brazil, made clear their opposition to any agreement unless the EC initiated farm subsidy reforms. In the face of EC opposition to such reforms, the talks collapsed in December 1990.

In general, there has been greater cooperation and harmony between US and Latin American negotiators than in most previous "rounds." The most important explanation for this harmony is the Latin American embrace of economic restructuring and open markets. President Bush's EAI is an added sweetener that has enhanced Latin America's cooperation on a range of Round issues. Some European cynics, however, have suggested that the US initiative is a tactic to force the EC to modify its protectionist CAP. As the chapters by Abugattas and Myles Frechette illustrate, there is a vast difference of opinion over the degree of cooperation that has taken place.

The failure to complete the Round in December 1990 reflects the new global economic and political realities. Europe no longer has the specter of Soviet power hanging over it. As a result, the US bargaining leverage has been reduced. Despite its economic global reach, Japan gave little leadership in the final December GATT negotiations, in part because of its desire to protect its agricultural sector, especially rice. Developing countries showed unexpected resolve—insisting that no agreement would be possible without fundamental agricultural reforms. Finally, for many senior US officials, a bad GATT agreement would be worse than none at all. Given the absence of goodwill by the key players, it is not surprising that the talks collapsed.

## Implications for Latin America

Latin America's continuing participation in the emerging global economic order will present unprecedented challenges to the region's leadership, as the concluding chapter by Carolyn Lamm points out. In the future, less reliance will have to be placed on geopolitical status, historical commitments, and third world solidarity. Rather, there is little choice but to find meaningful spaces or niches in the international economy and compete as heartily as possible. Latin American and Caribbean countries will have to market themselves more aggressively, especially in the capitals of the world where trade-related decisions are being made, such as Brussels and Geneva.

The likelihood of a US-Mexico-Canada free trade agreement has already diminished investor interest in the Caribbean and Central and South America.[31] Although early analysis suggests that trade and investment diversion should not be that great, any diversion away from the region can be ill-afforded at this critical point in the region's history.

Lessons from the CBI are instructive. One of the major reasons that it has not had the anticipated impact is that market access for Caribbean products has been insecure. But there are other reasons. Serious international investors in search of joint venture opportunities are conscious of the capacity and commitment of local private sectors to the national development of their respective countries. If the local private sector has little confidence in its own business environment, this feeling is quickly captured by potential new investors. Although there has been a generalized acceptance of open markets and reduced protectionism, the private sector's willingness in Latin America to accept the new reality of open markets has varied according to the country. While the idea of export processing zones seems to have been enthusiastically embraced, other measures of a fiscal and monetary nature have often been resisted, perhaps with good reason.

Sweeping transformations in communications technology and the resultant changes in international commercial law cannot be ignored by Latin America's leaders. Strategies must be found to understand and keep pace with the new infrastructure of global economic discourse. Ten years of negative economic growth during the last decade coupled with antiquated state ownership of the communications sector in the region puts it at a competitive disadvantage in the cellular age. Countries such as Guatemala and Venezuela, which otherwise offer some attractive conditions for foreign investors, are at a major competitive disadvantage with a phone system that simply does not work.

Latin America and the Caribbean will need to move rapidly in its effort to promote regional integration as a means to increase intraregional trade. Such a move would almost be a necessary prelude to entry into a

North American free trade area. Given the course of events and the new forces in the global economy, the longer the Caribbean and Central and South America remain outside of a trading relation with North America, the greater will be the effects of trade and investment diversion.

Thus, the post-Cold War era offers important new trade opportunities for the hemisphere. Nonetheless, even if such opportunities are seized through a combination of aggressive public and private sector leadership, other critical issues on the Latin American and Caribbean agenda will need attention: debt restructuring or forgiveness, the expansion of democratic rule, the reduction of urban and rural poverty and income inequality, and environmental protection. Expanded free trade in the hemisphere can be a means to a larger end; it cannot be an end in and of itself.

Education and awareness about the changing nature of the trade environment will be a critical feature of the hemisphere's ability to compete in global markets. This book is a modest effort to identify the critical components of change and the manner in which they interact. It is the product of a joint venture between the international law firm of White & Case and the Latin American and Caribbean Center of Florida International University. Such private-public ventures may be one feature of the hemisphere's effort to compete successfully. At the very minimum, it has provided both institutions with new perspectives on the advantages of working together for a common good.

## Notes

1. See *The Americas in a New World: The 1990 Report of the Inter-American Dialogue* (The Aspen Institute: The Inter-American Dialogue, 1991).

2. Norman Ornstein and Mark Schmitt, "Post-Cold War Politics," *Foreign Policy* 79 (Summer 1990): 174.

3. Henry Nau, "Domestic Trade Politics and the Uruguay Round: An Overview," in *Domestic Trade Politics and the Uruguay Round*, ed. Henry Nau (New York: Columbia University Press, 1989), xiii.

4. "The Enterprise for the Americas Initiative," Hearings before the Subcommittee on Human Rights and International Organizations, Western Hemisphere Affairs, and International Economic Policy and Trade of the Committee on Foreign Affairs, House of Representatives, June 28,

July 11, 18, 31, and September 27, 1990 (Washington, DC: US Government Printing Office, 1991).

5. See Anthony P. Gonzalez, "The View from the Caribbean," *Hemisphere* 3, no. 1 (Fall 1990): 26-28; "Caribbean Initiative" (Editorial), *Journal of Commerce*, 7 March 1991.

6. See George Grayson, "Mexico-Bashing in Washington," *Hemisphere* 1, no. 2 (Winter 1989): 45-48.

7. See Steven E. Sanderson, "Free Trade: Can Mexico Win?" *Hemisphere* 3, no. 2 (Winter/Spring 1991): 16-23.

8. See, for instance, "California Firms Air Concerns over a Mexico Trade Pact" and "US Labor Fights Mexico Trade Pact," *Journal of Commerce*, 6 February 1991; and "Group Seeks Reforms in Maquiladora Plants," *Journal of Commerce*, 13 February 1991.

9. US International Trade Commission, *The Likely Impact on the United States of a Free Trade Agreement with Mexico* (Washington, DC: US International Trade Commission, February 1991), vii.

10. Some analysts argue that the major problem in Canada has been of a macroeconomic nature—thus accelerating or being independent of the agreement with the US. For more information, see Nancy Riche, "Canadian Labor Speaks Out," and Ricardo Grinspun, "Free Trade Lessons from Canada," *Hemisphere* 3, no. 2 (Winter/Spring 1991): 26-30.

11. *International Business Chronicle*, 23 July-5 August 1990.

12. Leo Ryan, "Trade Talk from Canada," *Journal of Commerce*, 8 February 1991.

13. John Maggs, "Gephardt: Mexico Pact Must Cover such Topics as Labor, Environment," *Journal of Commerce*, 6 March 1991.

14. See Dory Owens, "Other Nations Fret over Free-Trade Pact," *The Miami Herald*, 24 October 1990; and Canute James, "Central America, Caribbean Fear Free-Trade Impact," *Journal of Commerce*, 11 December 1990.

15. In response to concerns that CBI countries might be early losers from any US-Mexico agreement, a number of proposals have been offered. First, Mexico could be required to open up its market to Caribbean products on a tariff-free basis under which these goods can then

enter the United States. Second, rules-of-origin in any US-Mexican agreement could permit Caribbean goods to be treated as if they originated in Mexico. Third, Mexico could permit Caribbean countries to transship their goods freely through Mexico, without administrative delays. See *Review of Trade and Investment Liberalization Measures by Mexico and Prospects for Future United States Mexican Relations: Phase II: Summary of Views on Prospects for Future United States Mexican Relations* (Washington, DC: United States International Trade Commission, October 1990), 1-29.

16. The trade agreement has three major components. The first is known as "asymmetrical reciprocity," which allows for a more rapid opening of the Mexican economy to Central American products. The second component stresses "multilateralism," which assures that products will move about through Central America free of barriers. A third component focuses on the general nature of the agreement, broadly encompassing all sectors of the economy. See *Centro-America Hoy*, 15 January 1991, 17.

17. See Jorge Salazar-Carrillo and Irma Alonso, "Mexico as a Potential Market for Central American and Caribbean Products" (Miami: Florida International University, 1990), 9-12.

18. See "Mexico—Key Player in Regional Trade Bloc," *Central America Report* XVIII, no. 2 (18 January 1991) and "Framework Trade Accord Strengthens Mexico's Role as 'US Intermediary,'" *Mexico and Central America Report*, 21 February 1991.

19. Alberto van Klaveren, "European-Latin American Relations in a World in Flux: From Optimism to Fatalism to Realism" (Prepared for a workshop of the Inter-American Dialogue, Airlie House, 23-25 May 1990); and Henry S. Gill, "Economic Implications for Latin America and the Caribbean of Changes in Eastern Europe" (Paper presented at the Conference on the Crisis in Eastern Europe: The Emerging New World Order and Its Implications for the Third World, Institute of International Relations, The University of the West Indies, St. Augustine, 9-10 May 1990).

20. Gonzalez, "The View from the Caribbean," loc. cit., 26.

21. Gill, "Economic Implications for Latin America and the Caribbean of Changes in Eastern Europe," loc. cit., 17.

22. Charles Gati, "East-Central Europe," *Foreign Affairs* 69, no. 5 (Winter 1990-91), 132-33.

23. Winston Fritsch, "Domestic Trade Reform and Policies towards the Trade System: Is There a Common Latin American Agenda?" (Prepared for the Working Group on Economics of the Inter-American Dialogue, May 1990), 13.

24. Charlotte Elton, "The New Japanese Presence in Central America: Challenges and Opportunities" (Washington, DC: XVI LASA Congress, 4-6 April 1991), 9-10.

25. About 41 percent of Latin America's exports to Japan were manufactured products—almost 75 percent of these are listed as semi-processed metals.

26. Panama has been used by the Japanese as a registry for its shipping fleet. Sales of ships to Panama-based Japanese companies inflate trade figures for Latin America. Without the large Japanese trade surplus with Panama, Japanese trade with Latin America would be in deficit, as the chapter by Stallings clearly points out.

27. Although *maquiladoras* are an exception, there has been little interest by either private sectors in Latin America. As Stallings has suggested elsewhere, "the irony is that U.S. stimulated liberalization in Japan has made it more difficult for the Japanese government to influence its private sector . . . thus making rivalry more likely and U.S. benefit from Japanese activity less." See Barbara Stallings, "Japan and Latin America: New Opportunities in the 1990s?" (Prepared for a workshop of the Inter-American Dialogue, Airlie House, 23-25 May 1990), 10.

28. The role of banking, insurance, information, transportation, and other services in the US economy and in international trade has expanded significantly in the last three decades. Services account for 70 percent of US gross national product and 75 percent of employment.

29. *Times of the Americas*, 22 August 1990, 9.

30. See also Acuerdo de Cartagena, *La iniciativa para las Américas del Presidente Bush: un desafío para América Latina y el Caribe* (Lima, September 1990), 9.

31. Interviews with knowledgeable specialists in the public and private sectors.

# 1

# Options for a Hemispheric Trade Order

*Gary C. Hufbauer and Jeffrey J. Schott\**

The constellation of trade arrangements has its own bright stars, red dwarfs, and black holes. The hugely successful European Community (EC) is a brilliant star; the problematic Uruguay Round at this writing is a red dwarf; the US-Mexico talks represent a young star; while the erstwhile Latin American Free Trade Area is a black hole. The question ahead is whether a shining new galaxy can be created for the Western Hemisphere.

We begin this chapter by reviewing the Enterprise for the Americas Initiative. We then look at the main trade arrangements among countries in the Western Hemisphere, and conclude by speculating on the configuration of a new Western Hemispheric trade order.

Our conclusions are straightforward. Past attempts at forging free trade agreements within Latin America failed because they did not meet certain obvious preconditions. These preconditions are now coming into place for selected Latin American countries, and the Enterprise for the Americas Initiative makes possible trade agreements with the United States. The result, in the first instance, will be a hub-and-spoke architecture, dealing with the most obvious border barriers. Eventually, this will be superseded by a "hub-spokes-rim" architecture and the agreements will be extended to reach behind the border barriers to domestic economic issues. As companion instruments to the trade agreements, social pacts will likely be devised, calling for better enforcement of existing health, safety, and environmental standards and requiring a gradual improvement in standards over time.

*\*Assisted by Magnus Lambsdorff, a research assistant at the Institute for International Economics.*

The timing of trade agreements will largely depend on external events. In particular, the Uruguay Round must come to a conclusion, and the US-Mexico Free Trade Agreement must be worked out, before far-reaching trade talks are possible with other Latin American nations.

## Enterprise for the Americas Initiative

On June 27, 1990, President Bush offered proposals for closer economic relations within the Western Hemisphere. Bush's Enterprise for the Americas Initiative (EAI) is broadly designed to support democratic governments and market-oriented reforms through a program that will cut trade barriers, promote investment, and help reduce debt.[1]

The trade arena is the centerpiece of the EAI, with the ultimate goal being the creation of a Western Hemisphere free trade zone. Assuming this goal is widely accepted in the United States and Latin America, the key issues are how long it will take to reach and the tactics by which it will be achieved.[2]

In the investment arena, the EAI seeks wholesale reform. According to Treasury Undersecretary David Mulford, only two or three Latin American and Caribbean nations currently maintain what the United States would consider an open investment regime.[3] In the debt arena, the EAI basically combines self-help with a modest amount of US assistance.

*Trade.* At this juncture, the EAI is short on trade specifics, but its general goals are clear. It presupposes that the Uruguay Round will succeed. According to the Bush administration, the EAI "is not an attempt by the United States to set up a regional trade bloc, but it is an effort to lower trade barriers in the region to the benefit of all trading nations."[4] Within the framework of the Uruguay Round, the United States has offered to assist Latin American countries in addressing specific trade issues, and has pledged support for tariff cuts on products of vital interest to Latin American exporters.

State Department policymakers have declared "that intra-regional trade barriers must fall and trade volume among Latin American countries and the Caribbean must jump before any country in the hemisphere other than Mexico and Chile will be ready to enter free trade talks with the United States."[5] As a first step, however, the United States has begun to negotiate bilateral framework agreements on trade and investment with a number of countries in the region. Seven countries—Bolivia, Chile, Colombia, Costa Rica, Ecuador, Honduras, and Mexico—already had signed such agreements by the end of 1990; talks are proceeding with Venezuela and the Southern Cone countries (Argentina, Brazil, Paraguay, and Uruguay); and the Andean Pact might well negotiate a framework agreement with the United States in 1992. The existing free trade agreement (FTA) with Canada, and the agreement now under discussion with Mexico, will presumably serve as models for substantive content when the framework agreements are succeeded by full-fledged trade agreements.

*Investment.* The EAI seeks to "help Latin American countries to compete for capital by reforming broad economic policies and specific regulatory systems."[6] To promote these objectives, the EAI proposes two new programs to be administered by the Inter-American Development Bank (IDB).

First, the IDB would create a new investment sectoral loan program to provide both technical advice and financial support for privatization efforts and liberalization of investment regimes—possibly coordinated with the World Bank. This program would enhance both IDB and World Bank sectoral lending facilities.

Second, the administration has proposed a multilateral investment fund, to which the United States, the EC, and Japan would each contribute $100 million annually over the next five years beginning in 1992. Additional contributions from other countries could boost the fund total to $2 billion. This sum, however, is comparatively small relative to the task at hand. The underlying diagnosis thus appears to be that policy reform is more important than cash.

The multilateral investment fund is designed to create a climate favorable to investment in Latin America, thereby attracting multiple amounts of private capital, including Latin American flight capital now residing in the United States and Europe. The fund would also promote investment reforms in the region, provide annual grants tied to these reforms, support efforts to privatize government-owned industries, and finance worker training, education, and health programs.

*External Debt.* Latin America's debt situation is still precarious.[7] At the end of 1990, the external debt outstanding totaled $423 billion. Most countries in the region have not kept current on their debt service and consequently ran up $11 billion in arrears in 1990.[8]

To deal with these debt issues, the EAI proposes that an Enterprise for the Americas Facility be administered by the Treasury Department in order to address debt reduction, investment reform, and environmental protection. The Facility will support debt reduction programs for countries that meet certain eligibility requirements set out in the proposed "Enterprise for the Americas Initiative Act of 1990" that are designed to promote a favorable investment climate:

1. The country should have an International Monetary Fund (IMF) standby arrangement, or an arrangement under the structural adjustment facility; in exceptional circumstances, the country should institute an IMF-monitored program or its equivalent.

2. The country should be receiving structural or sectoral loans from the World Bank or the International Development Association.

3. The country should have in place major investment reforms in conjunction with an IDB loan or it should be implementing an open investment regime.

4. The country should have negotiated a satisfactory financing program with commercial banks, including debt and debt service relief if appropriate.

When all these conditions are met, the United States would provide new payment terms for outstanding debt "extended under the Foreign Assistance Act of 1961 and credits extended pursuant to the Agricultural Trade Development and Assistance Act of 1954 (PL 480 aid)."[9] The agency whose loans or credits are affected will exchange—at the direction of the Facility—new obligations for obligations outstanding as of January 1, 1990. The principal and interest would be payable to the United States in US dollars.

Interest at concessionary rates, however, may be paid in local currency if the eligible country enters into a framework agreement establishing an Environmental Fund. This Fund would be jointly administered by the respective country and the US government to support local environmental projects. In the absence of an environmental agreement, interest would be paid in US dollars into a special account (the White House press release is ambiguous as to whether the account might be conditionally earmarked for the paying country). The EAI also calls for the sale, reduction, or cancellation of Eximbank loans and Commodity Credit Corporation (CCC) loans, provided the eligible country confirms that debt relief assistance will be used to carry out debt-for-equity or debt-for-nature swaps.

Latin American countries currently owe $12 billion to the US government. The Overseas Development Council has calculated that the total extent of the US debt initiative would, at maximum, amount to a savings in interest payments of about $400 million annually, if the total $12 billion were forgiven. If other countries of the Paris Club join the plan, this amount might rise to $1.6-2.3 billion—a fraction of the current annual net resource transfer out of Latin America, but significant in relation to what the Brady Plan has delivered so far.[10]

## Latin American Response

The EAI was warmly received throughout Latin America and the Caribbean. This reception reflects a fundamental change of economic and political thinking in Latin America. Economic policies of import-substitution and regulated markets are rapidly being replaced by policies of freer trade, hospitality to foreign investment, and extensive deregulation.

For example, Bolivia, Mexico, and Jamaica have dramatically and unilaterally liberalized their trade restrictions; Colombia and Costa Rica have made significant progress; and Argentina and Venezuela have initiated radical liberalization programs.[11] Even Peru and Brazil have now taken first steps to open their economies under new leaders elected in 1990. As a result of these reforms, more and more countries in the region have become able and willing to join the General Agreement on Tariffs and Trade (GATT). Chile, Peru, Argentina, Brazil, and Jamaica were already GATT members by 1979. Colombia joined in 1979; Mexico in 1986; Costa Rica became the 100th GATT signatory in November 1990; and ratification of Venezuela's protocol of accession is expected shortly.

The EAI is viewed as a chance to reap the benefits of recent economic reforms by expanding trade and improving economic efficiency. The EAI is further seen as a welcome change of US policy from an emphasis on military assistance and security considerations to an emphasis on closer economic relations.[12] Finally, some Latin American nations support the EAI as a defensive strategy to cope with the perceived risk of US protectionism (as did Canada), the feared decline of GATT authority, and the possible rise of an inward-looking European bloc.

Despite this general atmosphere of enthusiasm, there are concerns about the EAI's shortcomings and intentions. For example, Colombian finance minister Rudolf Hommes speculated that "the Initiative could introduce new economic inefficiencies by leading to a specialization of the productive basis of Latin American countries that is determined by the competitive advantage that may exist with relation to the United States or Canada, but would not necessarily exist with respect to the economies of the rest of the world."[13] Hommes criticized the overall proposal as not going far enough to facilitate the free movement of people, and the investment fund for being too small (compared, for example, to the European Bank for Reconstruction and Development, capitalized at $12 billion). Other observers fear that the EAI could become hostage to the bargaining strategies of commercial banks.[14] Furthermore, the environmental part of the EAI has received scant notice, partly because interest payments to the Environmental Fund would, at best, amount to about $50 million annually.

Overall, the trade part of the EAI has incited the most interest. The vision of a Western Hemisphere free trade zone is perceived as remarkable, overshadowing the investment and debt pillars.

## Existing Economic Integration Agreements in Latin America

If a new trade order is to emerge for the Western Hemisphere, it must draw on lessons derived from existing trade arrangements. Economic integration is a perennial topic in Latin America, and the list of bilateral and multilateral agreements is extensive. Owing to an array of economic and political obstacles, none of the initiatives has yet fulfilled its promise. There is no parallel within Latin America to the EC, or even to the European Free Trade Area.

Nevertheless, beginnings of integration within Latin America can be detected. Argentina and Brazil first embarked on sectoral trade integration and then entered into agreements aiming at overall trade integration. Mexico signed trade pacts with Chile and Venezuela in 1990. Existing trade groups, like the Andean Pact and the Caribbean Community, expanded earlier agreements.[15]

Only within the Southern Cone, however, has intra-regional trade growth been impressive, and that growth (68 percent between 1983 and 1989; see Table 1) largely took place before association talks began. Inside

## Table 1.  Regional Trade Flows in Latin America, 1983 and 1989

(millions of dollars)

| | 1983 | | | | 1989 | | | | % change from 1983 to 1989 | |
|---|---|---|---|---|---|---|---|---|---|---|
| | Imports | % of Total | Exports | % of Total | Imports | % of Total | Exports | % of Total | Imports | Exports |
| SOUTHERN CONE[a] | 22,410 | 100 | 31,021 | 100 | 26,265 | 100 | 55,358 | 100 | 17 | 78 |
| Intra-regional | 2,010 | 6 | 2,395 | 8 | 4,599 | 18 | 4,244 | 8 | 129 | 77 |
| Central America | 0 | 0 | 69 | 0 | 5 | 0 | 185 | 0 | n.a. | 169 |
| Andean Pact | 1,397 | 5 | 970 | 3 | 755 | 3 | 1,527 | 3 | (46) | 57 |
| CARICOM | 78 | 0 | 85 | 0 | 76 | 0 | 189 | 0 | (3) | 123 |
| United States | 3,670 | 12 | 6,098 | 20 | 6,276 | 24 | 9,741 | 18 | 71 | 60 |
| Mexico | 321 | 1 | 799 | 3 | 449 | 2 | 632 | 1 | 40 | (21) |
| Canada | 674 | 2 | 430 | 1 | 694 | 3 | 1,094 | 2 | 3 | 154 |
| Chile | 302 | 1 | 415 | 1 | 700 | 3 | 1,010 | 2 | 132 | 143 |
| All other | 13,959 | 45 | 19,761 | 64 | 12,712 | 48 | 36,737 | 66 | (9) | 86 |
| CENTRAL AMERICA[b] | 4,608 | 100 | 3,847 | 100 | 6,406 | 100 | 4,513 | 100 | 39 | 17 |
| Intra-regional | 684 | 15 | 749 | 19 | 571 | 9 | 723 | 16 | (17) | 3 |
| Southern Cone | 48 | 1 | 9 | 0 | 221 | 3 | 9 | 0 | 360 | 0 |
| Andean Pact | 281 | 6 | 114 | 3 | 423 | 7 | 37 | 1 | 51 | (68) |
| CARICOM | 175 | 4 | 54 | 1 | 35 | 1 | 37 | 1 | (80) | (31) |
| United States | 1,494 | 32 | 1,584 | 41 | 2,532 | 40 | 2,277 | 50 | 69 | 44 |
| Mexico | 442 | 10 | 31 | 1 | 375 | 6 | 30 | 1 | (15) | (2) |
| Canada | 73 | 2 | 29 | 1 | 86 | 1 | 181 | 4 | 17 | 517 |
| Chile | 7 | 0 | 1 | 0 | 11 | 0 | 0 | 0 | 51 | (67) |
| All other | 1,403 | 30 | 1,277 | 33 | 2,152 | 34 | 1,219 | 27 | 53 | (4) |

(continued)

**Table 1. (Continued) Regional Trade Flows in Latin America, 1983 and 1989**

(millions of dollars)

| | 1983 | | | | 1989 | | | | % change from 1983 to 1989 | |
|---|---|---|---|---|---|---|---|---|---|---|
| | Imports | % of Total | Exports | % of Total | Imports | % of Total | Exports | % of Total | Imports | Exports |
| ANDEAN PACT^c | 14,785 | 100 | 23,428 | 100 | 16,601 | 100 | 24,825 | 100 | 12 | 6 |
| Intra-regional | 909 | 6 | 809 | 3 | 796 | 5 | 1,130 | 5 | (12) | 40 |
| Central America | 56 | 0 | 267 | 1 | 38 | 0 | 407 | 2 | (32) | 52 |
| Southern Cone | 1,110 | 8 | 1,087 | 5 | 1,427 | 9 | 738 | 3 | 29 | (32) |
| CARICOM^d | 189 | 1 | 328 | 1 | 24 | 0 | 1,190 | 5 | (87) | 263 |
| United States | 5,924 | 40 | 8,654 | 37 | 6,432 | 39 | 11,732 | 47 | 9 | 36 |
| Mexico | 228 | 2 | 36 | 0 | 346 | 2 | 128 | 1 | 52 | 256 |
| Canada | 576 | 4 | 655 | 3 | 422 | 3 | 524 | 2 | (27) | (20) |
| Chile | 187 | 1 | 303 | 1 | 267 | 2 | 419 | 2 | 43 | 38 |
| All other | 5,606 | 38 | 11,289 | 48 | 6,849 | 41 | 8,557 | 34 | 22 | (24) |
| CHILE | 2,968 | 100 | 3,850 | 100 | 6,496 | 100 | 8,191 | 100 | 119 | 113 |
| Southern Cone | 421 | 14 | 292 | 8 | 1,146 | 18 | 630 | 8 | 172 | 115 |
| Central America | 0 | 0 | 0 | 0 | 0 | 0 | 12 | 0 | n.a. | n.a. |
| Andean Pact | 324 | 11 | 156 | 4 | 502 | 8 | 354 | 4 | 55 | 126 |
| United States | 704 | 24 | 1,083 | 28 | 1,283 | 20 | 1,616 | 20 | 82 | 49 |
| Mexico | 17 | 1 | 1 | 0 | 88 | 1 | 28 | 0 | 422 | n.a. |
| Canada | 61 | 2 | 60 | 2 | 142 | 2 | 56 | 1 | 133 | (7) |
| All other | 1,321 | 45 | 2,257 | 59 | 3,322 | 51 | 5,496 | 67 | 151 | 144 |

a Argentina, Brazil, Paraguay, and Uruguay.
b Costa Rica, El Salvador, Guatemala, Honduras, and Nicaragua.
c Bolivia, Colombia, Ecuador, Peru, and Venezuela.
d 13 Caribbean countries.

Sources: IMF, *Direction of Trade Statistics*, Yearbook 1990, Country Tables; US Department of Commerce, *US Trade 1990*.

the Andean Pact, trade declined by 12 percent between 1983 and 1989; within the Central American Common Market, trade decreased by 17 percent (see Table 1).[16] For some countries, the intra-regional export market in the late 1980s was of great importance—e.g., Bolivia (46%), Paraguay (30%), and Uruguay (26%)—but for most countries, Latin American markets are far less important than North American and European markets.

*The Andean Pact.* The Andean Pact was signed in 1969 in Cartagena by five Latin American nations: Bolivia, Colombia, Chile, Ecuador, and Peru. This agreement arose out of growing dissatisfaction with the existing Latin American Free Trade Area (LAFTA), which dated from 1960. In 1973, Venezuela entered the Andean Pact and, in 1976, Chile left the Pact.

Unlike LAFTA, which sought with little success to reduce tariffs on a product-by-product basis, the Andean Pact has freed three thousand items from tariffs for intra-bloc trade. Although a common external tariff has not been implemented, a degree of tariff harmonization was achieved through a minimum common external tariff. A 1990 study of the trade effects of the Andean Pact from 1968 to 1977 found annual trade creation of about 18.4 percent of total import values, offset by annual trade diversion of about 16.7 percent in the value of external imports.[17] Thus, the calculated net positive effect was only 1.7 percent annually, a fairly modest result.

Two phases of the Andean Pact can be observed. From 1970 to 1981, trade among member states grew at an average rate of 22 percent annually, reaching $1.2 billion. After 1981, however, trade declined within the region; and in 1989, intra-Andean imports amounted to about $800 million (excluding illicit drugs). Bilateral trade between Colombia and Venezuela accounted for 58 percent of that total. By contrast, trade with the United States in 1989 was about ten times greater than intra-Andean bloc trade (see Table 1).

Historically, Andean Pact policies toward foreign direct investment (FDI) have been less than liberal. The Andean nations placed special emphasis on a common policy toward FDI and technology transfer, fearing that the process of integration would promote geographic concentration of various industries disproportionately benefiting the advanced members. To counteract this anticipated result, particular industries were assigned to each country for the first ten years. Backing up the diversification policy, the Foreign Investment Code aimed at spreading the activities of multinational enterprise across all Andean members. The Code tried to allocate foreign investment to predetermined areas and industries. As a consequence of these regulations, investing firms—whether domestic or foreign—were not allowed to seek the highest prospective returns. This constraint contributed to an already weak investment climate resulting from macroeconomic mismanagement and political instability.[18]

The latest policy initiatives coming to the Andean region include US and EC attempts to promote legitimate commerce to deflect interest and participation in the drug trade, and the La Paz Agreement signed by five presidents, vowing to eliminate most of the interventionist provisions of the original Andean Pact.

In late 1990, the EC agreed to open unilaterally its market for certain Andean tropical products. The United States likewise agreed to give unilateral tariff preferences to most goods exported from Bolivia, Ecuador, Peru, and Colombia and to help farmers in the region reach global health and safety standards, improve certification procedures, and meet certain labeling requirements. After a seven-month US tariff review, however, only sixty-seven products—accounting for $27 million of merchandise exports—were made eligible for special tariff status under the Generalized System of Preferences (GSP).[19]

At a summit in La Paz on November 29-30, 1990, the five Andean Pact nations agreed to accomplish a true regional free trade area by 1992 by abolishing internal tariffs under the La Paz Agreement. The Andean countries have further agreed to establish common external tariff rates during 1991, and implement these rates by 1995, when a Andean customs union will be established. Meanwhile, all products will be eligible for tariff-free trade within the Andean area by December 31, 1991, and administered trade regimes will be abolished by 1992. Limits on private investment in strategic industries are to be eliminated by June 30, 1991. Regulations governing foreign investment, particularly those that prevent foreign investors from taking advantage of the free trade area, are to be modified before March 31, 1991.[20] These sweeping initiatives are designed to create a unified Andean economy not only for its own sake, but also to act as a substantial partner in negotiations with the United States.

*Central American Common Market.* The Central American Common Market (CACM) dates from the 1950s, achieved some results in the 1960s, but collapsed in the late 1970s. Lately, the CACM has been more of a paper creation than a force for integration.[21] The CACM members include El Salvador, Guatemala, Costa Rica, Honduras, and Nicaragua. Three of these countries—El Salvador, Guatemala, and Costa Rica—provide the bulk of total CACM trade, accounting for 92 percent of all exports within the area and for 84 percent of all imports from other member states. In the 1980s, ravaged by civil war and regional conflict, Central American economic integration retrogressed. Between 1984 and 1986, intra-regional trade decreased sharply (36 percent). While trade flows have recovered somewhat, the 1989 level of trade ($2.2 billion) was still below the 1983 level ($2.3 billion).

CACM exports to the other two trade associations, the Andean Pact and the Caribbean Community, were lower in 1989 than 1983. By contrast, trade with the United States has grown sharply and accounts for almost half of the region's total trade (see Table 1). Between 1983 and 1989, CACM exports to the United States rose from $1.6 billion to $2.3 billion, while CACM imports from the United States more than tripled from $1.5 billion to $4.8 billion (reflecting sharply higher military purchases).

Then, in January 1991, CACM members agreed to negotiate sectoral free trade pacts with Mexico as part of a broader program (including concessionary oil sales) to strengthen bilateral economic relations.[22]

*Caribbean Community.* The Caribbean Community (CARICOM), founded in 1973, includes thirteen English-speaking Caribbean nations with a population of 5.5 million.[23] From 1981 to 1986, persistent shortages of foreign exchange—due to weak export prices and volumes for petroleum, bauxite, and sugar—prompted a considerable decline in intra-regional trade. Member trade, however, has expanded since 1987, increasing by 20 percent in 1989 to reach $317 million.[24]

In a meeting in October 1990 in Kingston, Jamaica, the leaders of CARICOM continued to emphasize further economic integration as a means to deal with emerging regional trading blocs in North America, Europe, and Southeast Asia. CARICOM may enlarge by accepting new members, such as Haiti, Surinam, and the Dominican Republic. Leaders also agreed on a common external tariff, effective April 1, 1991, with special provisions worked out for vulnerable sectors. Moreover, in 1991, new rules will allow duty-free and restriction-free movement of CARICOM-produced goods between the member states.[25] Finally, the CARICOM Stock Exchange is scheduled to open by January 1, 1992; and, by 1994, leaders hope to have achieved currency alignment among member states.[26]

US-Caribbean trade relations have not yet fulfilled the expectations that were raised by the Caribbean Basin Initiatives of Presidents Reagan (CBI I) and Bush (CBI II). These initiatives essentially promised one-way free trade, but nearly all products of current commercial interest to the Caribbean nations were excluded. Since 1983, total exports of CARICOM to the United States have in fact been halved, from $4.6 billion to only $2.3 billion annually. Other factors were also at work, but the two CBIs did not noticeably help increase the Caribbean states' exports to the United States. CARICOM still seeks duty-free and quota-free concessions on exports to the United States of so-called "sensitive" items: textiles and apparel, leather products, sugar, and fruits and vegetables.

*Southern Cone.* The Southern Cone—composed of Argentina, Brazil, Paraguay, and Uruguay—seems to be in the process of reformation. In April 1988, Presidents José Sarney of Brazil and Raúl Alfonsín of Argentina signed an industrial complementary agreement to coordinate policies in their auto, food, aircraft, and other industries. Since then, the pace of integration has increased, and new bilateral and multilateral agreements are in the making. In July 1990, the new leaders of Argentina and Brazil, Presidents Carlos Menem and Fernando Collor de Mello, respectively, agreed to form a common market by the end of 1994. Recently, Uruguay and Paraguay indicated that they would be interested in joining an integrated Southern Cone market. These announcements . came only a few days after President Bush proposed the EAI.

Trade within the Southern Cone grew by 129 percent between 1983 and 1989, while Southern Cone imports from the Andean Pact decreased by 46 percent, and from CARICOM by 3 percent. On the other side of the ledger, the Southern Cone countries exported more to these countries in 1989 than in 1983. They also boosted their trade with the United States by more than 60 percent.

Chile has been mentioned as a possible member of the Southern Cone subregion, but more likely Chile will "go it alone" through negotiations with the United States. Chile has outpaced all the other countries in the region in the speed of its economic reforms, and prefers to negotiate a FTA with the United States far more quickly than would be possible if it had to wait for its neighbors to catch up. Chilean efforts seem to be bearing fruit. During his visit to Chile in December 1990, President Bush put prospective FTA talks on the near-term agenda, and US trade representative Carla Hills reinstated Chile as a beneficiary under the GSP.[27]

# US-Canada Free Trade Agreement[28]

The US free trade agreement with Canada[29] will inevitably serve as a reference point both for talks with Mexico and for wider hemispheric negotiations. Given the disparities in income between the United States and Latin American countries, however, one should not expect bold progress on trade liberalization comparable to the US-Canada FTA. Moreover, based on the Canadian precedent, Latin American nations should not expect an FTA to come into place quickly, or to instantly solve their economic ills.

The United States and Canada had substantial economic ties before entering bilateral trade negotiations. In 1986, US merchandise exports to Canada accounted for 25 percent of total US exports, and US imports from Canada accounted for 19 percent of total US imports. Trade ties were even more substantial from the Canadian perspective. Canadian merchandise exports to the United States accounted for 77 percent of Canadian exports, and imports accounted for 67 percent.[30] Comparable dependence on US commercial ties is evident for Mexico (see Table 2). For Chile and the Southern Cone of Latin America, trade with the United States is about 20 percent of total trade, while for the rest of Latin America the figure approaches 50 percent (see Table 1).

The Shamrock Summit between President Reagan and Prime Minister Brian Mulroney in March 1985, in Quebec City, set both countries on the track toward bilateral trade liberalization. The broad goal was to establish a climate of predictability and confidence for Canadian and American firms alike to plan, invest, grow, and compete more effectively with one another and in the global market. After more than a century of false starts, US-Canadian FTA negotiations began fourteen months after they were first broached and then took another seventeen months to conclude;[31] even then, some issues still proved so sensitive that the agreement fell short of expectations (notably in transportation services, intellectual property, and "unfair" trade remedies).

Any trade agreements between the United States and Latin American countries will likewise take time to negotiate; and, inevitably difficult and sensitive issues will arise. The following paragraphs summarize key elements of the US-Canada FTA.

### Table 2. Mexico's Regional Trading Partners, 1980 and 1989

(% of total trade)

|  | 1980 | 1989[a] | 1980 | 1989[a] |
|---|---|---|---|---|
| United States | 64.7 | 63.3 | 61.6 | 67.0 |
| Canada | 0.8 | 2.4 | 1.8 | 1.8 |
| Japan | 4.3 | 7.1 | 5.1 | 5.3 |
| Other industrial countries | 15.6 | 16.3 | 17.3 | 16.3 |
| Latin America and Caribbean | 6.9 | 5.2 | 4.2 | 4.2 |
| Other developing countries | 5.8 | 3.6 | 1.6 | 2.4 |
| Other[b] | 2.0 | 2.1 | 8.3 | 3.1 |

[a]Estimated.
[b]USSR and other non-members.

Sources: IMF, *Direction of Trade Statistics*, Yearbook 1987 and 1990.

*Tariffs.* The US-Canada FTA seeks to eliminate all tariffs between the two countries over a ten-year period. Tariffs on some products were eliminated immediately, but most tariffs were scheduled to be eliminated over five to ten years in equal annual installments. Since the FTA went into force, however, both countries have agreed to accelerate tariff cuts on a broad range of products during two subsequent tariff reviews. The FTA has thus fortified the momentum for trade reform. The US-Canada pattern of tariff liberalization sets a good standard for a broader Western Hemisphere compact, although in many cases the cuts would need to be phased asymmetrically: larger cuts in the early years by the United States.

*Government Procurement.* The FTA expanded on obligations that both countries had already undertaken in the GATT Code on Government Procurement. It also lowered the threshold of the contract value from

$171,000 to $25,000 for the application of competitive bidding procedures and other GATT rules.

*Energy.* The FTA contains commitments not to impose restrictions on imports and exports—including quotas, taxes, or price requirements—with limited exceptions for national security and short supply circumstances. It thereby guarantees market access for Canadian producers, and reliable supplies for US consumers. The energy security issue will undoubtedly take on added importance in the aftermath of the Persian Gulf Crisis.

*Agriculture.* The FTA eliminated agricultural tariffs and removed some non-tariff barriers, but major farm policies in each country were left unchanged—supposedly to be reformed through Uruguay Round talks. The inclusion of agricultural liberalization in future regional trade pacts will depend on the extent of reforms reached in GATT talks.

*Investment.* The FTA eliminated the screening requirements for most US greenfield investments, and indirect US acquisitions in Canada. By 1992, the threshold for screening direct acquisitions will be increased, so that it will only apply to the top 600-plus Canadian firms. Moreover, the FTA bars the introduction of new trade-related performance requirements, but important exemptions to several of these provisions limit their application to the energy and cultural sectors.

*Automotive Trade.* Under the FTA, Canada agreed to eliminate immediately its export-based duty remission scheme, to phase out its production-based incentive scheme by 1995, to remove its embargo on used car imports within five years, and to not extend the benefits of the Auto Pact to new companies that establish assembly plants in Canada. The FTA also increased somewhat the North America content rule that must be met for a company to benefit from bilateral duty-free trade.

*Resolution of Subsidy/Countervail and Antidumping Problems.* Much to the disappointment of Canada, no new rules were reached on the application of countervailing duties (CVD) and antidumping duties (ADD). The FTA committed both countries to continue negotiating a harmonized regime on subsidies/CVD and ADD over a five to seven-year period. The FTA also established ex post procedures to resolve disputes about the consistency of final CVD and ADD orders with existing national laws and GATT obligations. Disputes on subsidy/CVD and ADD issues are subject to binding arbitration.

*Services.* The FTA created a framework of rights and obligations regarding national treatment, establishment, and licensing and certification procedures. In addition, FTA provisions facilitate the temporary cross-border movement of professional workers (the only provisions relating to trade in labor services). Most existing restrictions were "grandfathered," although significant liberalization was achieved in the financial services sector. The FTA removed restrictions on US banks— notably the 16-percent limit on total banking assets that foreign subsidiaries may hold in the Canadian market—and relaxed a restrictive rule on US insurance groups operating in Canada.

*Dispute Settlement.* The FTA established a Canada-US Trade Commission, composed of trade minsters and their representatives, to supervise the operation of the FTA and to resolve all disputes except those relating to subsidy/CVD and ADD matters (which are handled through their own arbitration mechanism) and financial services (which are handled through a consultative system between the US Treasury and the Canadian Department of Finance).

## The Road to a North American Free Trade Area

In February 1991 President Bush announced that the United States, Canada, and Mexico will begin negotiations on a North American Free Trade Area (NAFTA). Coming on the heels of the US-Canada FTA (ratified in 1989), the US-Mexico trade and investment pact (signed October 1989), and the Canada-Mexico framework agreement (signed in March 1990), the prospective US-Canada-Mexico talks have broad implications for economic relations between the three countries of North America. Negotiations will likely begin in the spring of 1991, assuming Congress consents to the applicability of fast-track procedures to implement the prospective pact. An agreement then would probably be ready by the spring of 1992.

**Goals of the Partners.** Mexico, Canada, and the United States each have their own reasons for pursuing a NAFTA. The degree of complementariness will largely determine the scope and pace of talks.

*Mexico.* As the smallest and most protected economy, Mexico has the most to gain over time from a NAFTA. An agreement would reinforce and accelerate the pace of domestic reforms currently under way, and would guarantee access to the broader North American market. Further, an open trade policy could help alleviate Mexico's crippling debt service burden, and help finance the current account deficit by encouraging foreign direct investment and the return of flight capital (statistics on Mexican trade patterns appear in Table 2).

*Canada.* Canadian interests in a NAFTA are more defensive than Mexican interests. Canada wants to maintain its position as a player in the dialogue between Mexico and the United States, to safeguard Canadian rights under the US-Canada FTA, and to deal with such questions as trade in automobiles and parts and natural gas flows. In some instances, Canada and Mexico may find common commercial interests juxtaposed against the United States.

*The United States.* US interests are both political and economic. Economic growth should promote a stable and democratic regime in Mexico, providing a good model for other countries in the region. The FTA would reinforce ongoing trade and investment reforms in Mexico, and thus likely contribute to increased economic growth. Many Fortune 500 manufacturing firms are looking to the global advantages of safe investment and production in Mexico. A prosperous Mexico would become a thriving market for US exports, providing a particular boost to the economies of border states such as California, Texas, New Mexico, and Arizona. At the same time, growth in the Mexican economy would create new jobs and increase wages in Mexico, and thus help stem the tide of illegal immigration. Finally, in the face of a rapidly integrating EC, a NAFTA has political appeal in showing that "we can do it, too."

For both Canada and the United States, however, an economic partnership with a low-wage country of nearly 90 million people could have enormous consequences. Labor-intensive and machine-driven industries in Canada and the United States—fruits and vegetables, textiles, automobiles and parts, household equipment, and consumer electronics—could significantly contract over a period of ten or fifteen years. On the other hand, Canada and the United States should greatly gain from increased exports of sophisticated products and services to Mexico, and from the ability to draw on Mexican labor and resources to compete in world markets.

*Impact on Third Countries.* Estimates indicate that, over a five-year period, trade creation of a US-Mexico agreement, coming on top of the US-Canada FTA, will greatly outweigh trade diversion.[32] Eliminating US tariffs on Mexican products would increase Mexican exports to the United States by about $1.4 billion in the early 1990s; and eliminating both tariff and non-tariff barriers would increase Mexican exports by about $2.8 billion. Mexican exports of clothing, machinery, transportation equipment, and fruits and vegetables will especially benefit from the trade pact. Total trade diversion would probably not exceed $0.4 billion. The diversion effect on Central and South America is estimated, at worst, at under $0.2 billion. If sector-specific deals on non-tariff barriers come at the expense of third country suppliers, however, the diversion effect could become much more pronounced.

*Agenda.* The agenda for both the bilateral US-Mexico agreement and the trilateral NAFTA will likely follow the model of the US-Canada FTA, including negotiations on specific sectoral issues. Broader economic issues such as monetary integration and labor mobility will be excluded from an agreement. Nevertheless, US labor unions and environmental and consumer groups are pressing for the inclusion of social issues involving environmental, work-place, health, and safety standards, as well as drug trafficking.

*Tariffs and Quotas.* Mexico has reduced its average weighted tariff to about 10 percent, set a maximum rate of 20 percent, and has substantially harmonized its tariff schedule. The United States already extends tariff preferences to Mexico under the Generalized System of Preferences and HTS categories 9802.00.60 and 9802.00.80 (formerly TSUS 806.30 and 807.00, provisions that underpin *maquiladora* operations). Non-tariff barriers likely to be targeted for liberalization include: US steel quotas (in case they do not expire as scheduled in March 1992); Mexican local content and export requirements in the auto industry; and both US and Mexican quotas in agriculture, textiles, and apparel. These sectors, of course, will also be targeted by opponents of trade liberalization in an effort to derail trade talks entirely or at least exempt the sectors from coverage. In addition, questions remain concerning the timing of tariff phase-outs and special treatment for affected industries.

*Agriculture.* This sector is beset by layers of barriers in the form of tariffs, quotas, and phytosanitary regulations. The United States has a wide number of specific duties on fruits and vegetables, which range up to 38 percent ad valorem. Both the United States and Mexico also impose extensive import licensing controls on agricultural products. The US quotas are hard on sugar, fruits and vegetables (fourteen commodities are subject to marketing orders with a strong seasonal component); Mexican quotas are hard on US grain exports, especially during the Mexican harvest season. The United States is worried both about Mexican pests and animal diseases making their way north and about pesticide levels on crops.

*Energy.* The energy sector holds the greatest promise for big new US investment, but is politically explosive for Mexico. The government has owned and controlled the energy sector since 1938. Mexico desperately needs foreign capital to upgrade aging machinery and gain technology to exploit difficult new fields. With rising domestic consumption and flat or declining production, Mexico could become an oil importer by the year 2000 in the absence of major new investments. The recent $1.5 billion Eximbank loan—possibly expanding to $6.5 billion over the next few years—gives American oil-service companies access to Mexican oil-development projects.[33] Nevertheless, it remains an open question whether Mexico can attract participation by foreign companies with the advanced technologies needed to explore and exploit its oil reserves; US oil companies rankle because they are still prohibited from direct equity investment in the Mexican oil industry.

*Automotive Industry.* Mexico has a highly regulated automobile industry. FTA negotiators are likely to discuss issues such as safety standards in factories; import restrictions under the 1989 Mexican Auto Decree (which limits imports to 15 percent of domestic sales in 1991 and 1992); export requirements (exports must be a multiple of imports, 1.75 by 1994); value-added requirements (36 percent local content to be supplied by locally owned firms); and investment limitations. The 1989 Decree has been applauded by auto producers, but is disliked by US and Canadian auto parts manufacturers. The interaction between the US-Mexico FTA and the US-Canada Auto Pact raises fears in Canada that the whole industry will move south. The key element in the negotiations will thus involve the establishment of common rules of origin.

*Services.* An agreement on services would build on the model of the US-Canada FTA and on the provisions of the prospective General Agreement on Trade in Services (GATS) that is being developed in the Uruguay Round. The GATS will likely contain a framework of rights and obligations that stress transparency of regulations and the application of the national treatment principle, and that liberalize trade through an evolutionary process, sector by sector, starting from the base line of existing policies. All this is facilitated by Mexican privatization of its banking and telecommunications sectors.

*Maquiladora.* *Maquiladoras* have drawn criticism from factions both within the United States and Mexico. Problems include: low average wages in Mexico; exploitation of young and female workers; low unionization; and inadequate health and safety standards in the work place. These issues are likely to be revisited in prospective US negotiations with other countries or regions in the hemisphere. *Maquila* operations, however, offer two benefits for the United States: *maquila* imports are an alternative to goods from East Asia and lead to a larger back flow of US exports to Mexico, and *maquilas* reduce emigration to the United States by providing jobs for about 440,000 Mexicans.

*Countervailing Duty and Antidumping Laws.* Prospective results in the Uruguay Round do not hold great promise for reforming the multilateral GATT rules that govern national CVD and ADD proceedings. Given the experience of the US-Canada talks, bilateral and regional pacts will likewise only be able to make small, incremental reforms. An agreement on CVD and ADD could start, however, by including a dispute settlement procedure along lines similar to the US-Canada FTA procedures. Over time, the ADD regime could be supplemented, and eventually supplanted by a common competition policy standard. In the distant future, it might be possible to negotiate a NAFTA code limiting domestic subsidies, as well as export subsidies, so that CVD proceedings dwindle in number and importance.

## Lessons for the Hemisphere

The successes and failures of past trade agreements suggest various lessons for new efforts to achieve free trade within the hemisphere. Those lessons can be grouped under three headings: preconditions, timing, and subject matter.

*Preconditions for a Trade Agreement.* More often than not, free trade agreements are concluded between countries with similar levels of per capita income. Many social conditions correlate with per capita income: for example, general wage levels, minimum wage legislation, health and safety rules for the work place, social safety nets (old age, health, and welfare assistance), environmental controls, and educational standards. When such social conditions are similar, the trauma of economic integration is much reduced. In two major instances of pronounced social disparities, the richer partner agreed to help the poorer partner with very substantial flows of financial assistance. Thus, when the EC was enlarged to include Greece, Spain, and Portugal, a massive regional assistance program was inaugurated to improve the infrastructure in poorer parts of Europe. Likewise, when the German Democratic Republic was reunited with the Federal Republic, the Federal Republic committed huge amounts of money to a broad reconstruction program.

Obviously, per capita income disparities between the United States and Latin American nations are great: more than a factor of ten in the case of the United States and Mexico. It is most unlikely that large-scale financial assistance programs will be devised to bridge the ensuing social disparities. Other solutions will have to be devised.

In addition to finding imaginative solutions to ease concerns about vast social disparities, five preconditions will need to be met before worthwhile trade agreements can be negotiated between the United States and single Latin American nations or groups of countries. When those conditions are met, then a trade agreement can act as an archstone holding together the pillars of a functioning, growth-oriented economy.

The first precondition is a reasonable degree of monetary stability. Experience teaches that high *average* inflation rates, year-to-year, are also *highly variable* rates, year-to-year. Highly variable inflation wrenches and twists the economy: not all prices and wages rise and fall at the same rate. In particular, with high and variable inflation, enormous shifts in the real exchange rate are bound to occur (see Table 3), which alternately exposes the traded goods sector to mania and depression. In manic episodes, partner countries will inevitably complain about unfair trade subsidized by a cheap exchange rate; in depressive moods, home country industries will certainly seek, and often obtain, protection against imports. This was the experience of the United States in the first half of the 1980s, when a rapid fall in inflation and a super strong dollar led to a wave of protection in automobiles, steel, and other products. It is a recurring experience in Latin America.

**Table 3. Quantitative Indicators of Preconditions for Entry into a Free Trade Agreement, 1987-89**

| | Average inflation rate | Average change in real effective exchange rate | Taxes on int'l transactions (% total revenue) |
|---|---|---|---|
| United States | 2.8 | 5.4 | 1.7 |
| Canada | 3.3 | 9.7 | 3.8 |
| Australia | 6.0 | 9.0 | 4.6 |
| New Zealand | 5.4 | 6.2 | 2.8 |
| European Community | | | |
| Belgium | 1.5 | 4.2 | 0.0 |
| Denmark | 3.4 | 4.4 | 0.1 |
| France | 2.2 | 2.7 | 0.3 |
| Germany | 1.4 | 0.6 | 0.0 |
| Greece | 13.9 | 1.7 | 3.3 |
| Ireland | 2.2 | n.a. | 3.6 |
| Italy | 4.3 | 2.3 | 0.0 |
| Luxembourg | 1.6 | 0.5 | 0.1 |
| Netherlands | 0.6 | 2.2 | 0.0 |
| Portugal | 9.5 | 3.2 | 1.9 |
| Spain | 4.6 | 4.6 | 2.8 |
| United Kingdom | 4.7 | 4.8 | 0.1 |
| Mexico | over 100.0 | 11.9 | 3.4 |
| Andean Pact (ANCOM) | | | |
| Bolivia | 48.0 | 4.6 | 12.6 |
| Colombia | 29.9 | 3.5 | 11.2 |
| Ecuador | 94.5 | 18.4 | n.a. |
| Peru | over 100.0 | 14.3 | 21.5 |
| Venezuela | 66.0 | 14.0 | 23.4 |
| Central American Common Market (CACM) | | | |
| El Salvador | 22.5 | n.a. | 21.1 |
| Guatemala | 12.0 | n.a. | 37.2 |
| Honduras | 5.3 | n.a. | n.a. |
| Costa Rica | 17.8 | 6.0 | 21.1 |
| Nicaragua | n.a. | 20.3 | 16.9 |
| Southern Cone | | | |
| Brazil | over 100.0 | 16.8 | 1.6 |
| Argentina | over 100.0 | 13.2 | 10.3 |
| Uruguay | over 100.0 | 5.1 | 13.6 |
| Paraguay | 29.4 | 14.1 | 12.0 |
| Chile | 16.3 | 4.3 | 9.9 |

(continued)

Table 3. (Continued) Quantitative Indicators of Preconditions for Entry into a Free Trade Agreement

| | Average inflation rate | Average change in real effective exchange rate | Taxes on int'l transactions (% total revenue) |
|---|---|---|---|
| Selected Caribbean Economic Community | | | |
| Bahamas | 3.7 | 1.8 | 58.0 |
| Barbados | 4.0 | n.a. | 13.8 |
| Cayman Islands | n.a. | n.a. | 42.1 |
| Guyana | 27.8 | 25.6 | 10.0 |
| Jamaica | 9.7 | n.a. | 4.1 |
| Netherlands Antilles | 2.3 | 3.9 | 24.4 |
| St. Kitts & Nevis | 1.8 | n.a. | 26.0 |
| St. Lucia | 1.9 | 4.1 | 33.6 |
| St. Vincent | n.a. | 3.1 | 43.6 |

Sources: IMF, *Government Finance Statistics Yearbook*, 1990; JP Morgan, *World Financial Markets*, July 1990; IMF, *International Financial Statistics*, November 1990.

The second precondition is a willingness to accept the tenets of a market economy and to reject the teachings of statism. Possibly the most important effect of lowered trade barriers is increased competitive pressure on domestic industry. Such pressure is stoutly resisted by state-run firms, which are usually the victim of two forces. First, employees and managers come to think of themselves as tenured workers. In turn, this makes it necessary to maintain output, even when the goods are rejected by the market; and it makes it hard to introduce efficiencies that entail staff layoffs. Second, cozy relations develop with domestic supplying industries, and these relations virtually equate to buy-national preferences. When a large part of industry operates under state control, free trade is at best a nuisance. Neither on the production side nor on the purchasing side do state enterprises wish to respond to market signals, and their first line of defense will be to block those signals by undermining the trade agreement.

On an index from zero (backsliding toward statism) to four (embrace of private markets), some Latin American countries may be scored as follows for their performance in the 1980s. In the category of four are Chile and Mexico (the amazing transition from José López Portillo to Carlos Salinas de Gortari); in the category of three: Costa Rica, Jamaica,

Bolivia, Venezuela, and Argentina; in the category of two: Colombia; in the category of one: Brazil; in the category of zero: Peru.[34] A more recent report card on government policies and officials, based on evaluations of corporate executives and analysts, leads to the following scores for 1990: Chile and Mexico, three; Brazil, Colombia, and Venezuela, high two; Argentina, Peru, Ecuador, and Uruguay, low two.[35] Evidently, 1990 elections in both Brazil and Peru installed new regimes that moved each country up the scale.

The third precondition is an ability and willingness of the government to look to other revenue sources than imposts on international transactions. When import tariffs and export taxes form a large part of government revenues, it will be very difficult for governments to accept even the first step in any trade agreement that looks to the phase-out of these charges. As Table 3 shows, Latin American countries vary enormously in their dependence on import tariffs and export taxes.

The fourth precondition is trade linkage. At least one of the partner countries needs to depend significantly on trade with the other. This dependence establishes the raison d'être for the negotiation, that is, to receive preferential trade treatment in order to secure and expand access to the partner's market. The clearest examples of this point are in North America, where both Canada and Mexico rely on the US market for the preponderant share of their trade.

The final precondition, vital in any trade agreement with the United States (or the EC, for that matter), is a functioning democracy. Within the United States, there will always be economic opponents to a free trade agreement. These opponents will usually be able to carry the day against proposed concessions to a dictator or a military government. Moreover, the United States has a long history of applying economic sanctions against Latin American nations (twenty-five cases since World War II).[36] A trade agreement with a dictatorship will often be at risk of interruption by the United States.

Sometimes, as in the US-Canada agreement, or the Australia-New Zealand agreement, these five preconditions have been in place for a very long period before the trade agreement was reached. But that need not always be the case. The idea of the EC gathered force in the early 1950s, only a few years after World War II and the rule of fascism in Germany and Italy. In Europe, the Treaty of Rome was seen as the archstone of a democratic peaceful continent, and a way to lock in liberal economic and political institutions. Similarly, the US-Mexico FTA, if it succeeds, will come into place when monetary stability is a recent achievement in Mexico, and just as statism is being dismantled. We take the view that a long record of democracy, free markets, and monetary stability is not required. Instead, the focus should be on recent events, and on *trends* as much as *levels*. Even so, conditions are radically different from country to country, which brings us to issues of timing.

*Timing.* In his June 27, 1990, speech launching the EAI, President Bush stated that he is willing to negotiate with every single country on a bilateral basis, or if possible with groups of countries. But not everything can be done at once. There are two main timing issues. The first is the time sequence between hemispheric negotiations and US-Mexico and NAFTA negotiations. The second is the priority of countries or country groups in their negotiations with the United States. Taken together, timing considerations point, in the first instance, to a "hub-and-spoke" model rather than a "hub-spoke-rim" model. In a "hub-and-spoke" model, the United States is the "hub" while Canada, Mexico, and later individual Latin American countries are the "spokes." Only when the "spokes" join together will there be a "hub-spoke-rim" system.

In the best of all possible worlds, free trade would be achieved through a single plurilateral trade agreement rather than separate bilateral pacts between the United States, Canada, Mexico, and other countries in the region. Ronald Wonnacott argues that the bilateral approach will create a "discriminatory, inefficient, hub-and-spoke trading structure" that would benefit the United States (the "hub") more than its trading partners (the "spokes"), and could erode prospects for future multilateral liberalization.[37]

But Wonnacott's argument is a case of the best being the enemy of the good. The logic for starting with a hub-and-spoke system is the "drop-lock" argument. At different times, different Latin American countries will meet the preconditions for a worthwhile agreement. If the moment is not seized, there may well be policy retrogression. Moreover, it is unlikely that the preconditions will be met for a large group of Latin American countries at a single point in time in the near to medium term.

There is much to be said for delaying substantive hemispheric trade talks until the North American FTA is wrapped up sometime in 1992. This short delay, while framework agreements are being implemented (see below), will allow countries in Latin America a better opportunity to achieve the preconditions for a meaningful trade agreement. Moreover, in political terms, the United States can only digest so much trade liberalization within a two-year time frame. US-Mexico talks are sure to provoke the US fruit and vegetable and textile industries; and other US industries, notably petroleum and automobiles, will be watching carefully to see whether they are getting from Mexico as much as they "deserve." The political circuits might well be overloaded by the simultaneous negotiation of free trade agreements with additional Latin American countries.

But that does not mean a halt to diplomatic initiatives for the next two years. Seven Latin American nations have already signed bilateral trade and investment agreements with the United States; Brazil, Argentina, Paraguay, and Uruguay are wrapping up the remaining details for similar framework agreements;[38] the CARICOM countries have experience with two CBIs; and the Andean Pact might negotiate a framework agreement in 1992. These agreements are essential precursors for trade negotiations. The question ahead is the priority sequence of countries and country groups for full-fledged free trade talks. There are two that stand out in readiness terms: Chile and the CARICOM nations.

As a single medium-sized country, Chile is the most obvious candidate. Chile has expressed a keen interest in talks with the United States. Democracy, free markets, monetary stability, and low reliance on tariffs all characterize Chile. In his December 1990 visit to Santiago, President Bush proclaimed "Chile has moved further, faster than any other nation in South America toward real free-market reform" and declared the country a prime candidate for debt relief under the EAI.[39]

The CARICOM group is also eager for a free trade arrangement. The main obstacle is US reluctance to grant duty-free concessions on US imports of "sensitive products"—textiles, petroleum products, footwear, and leather goods—as part of the revised Caribbean Basin Initiative (CBI II). These issues are still on the table and the Caribbean nations are also seeking an expansion of the US quota for sugar.[40] A further obstacle within the CARICOM nations is its high revenue reliance on taxes on international transactions (see Table 3). With these sizeable caveats, the CARICOM group meets the preconditions for a trade agreement.

*Subject Matter.* Broadly speaking, the US-Canada FTA provides the best guide to the *ultimate* content of trade agreements negotiated between the United States and Latin American nations. But the commitments by Mexico under the NAFTA agreement will probably provide the best guide to the *first stage* of future agreements with Latin American countries.

In the first stage, tariffs will be phased out over periods not longer than ten years; but in some cases the cuts will be asymmetric (that is, faster for the United States) and extended in duration, say to fifteen years. Predictably, once the phase-out is agreed, accelerations will be negotiated. Quotas will also be liberalized, but here idiosyncratic formulas with ample safeguards will be negotiated sector by sector. In addition, the first stage will establish a framework for dispute settlement, common rules of origin, and administrative procedures, consistent with the US-Canada FTA.

Beyond that, other items may be postponed to later stages, but not indefinitely. In large part, the US agenda will consist of unfinished business from the Uruguay Round: intellectual property protection; rules against distortions to investment (local content and export performance requirements); national treatment for services; and better discipline on subsidies.

On a longer timetable, the negotiators will address key social issues: environment, wages, and labor standards.[41] Already now, on the eve of NAFTA negotiations, US fears are focused on the *maquiladoras* in Mexico. Lower wages and lax health and safety standards are luring companies into border plants. The environmental issues of hazardous waste disposal, sewage treatment by border cities such as Tijuana, local air pollution and greenhouse gases, and saline water flowing from the United States to Mexico cannot be indefinitely postponed. Our guess is that, if trade agreements go forward with Mexico and other Latin American nations, they will be accompanied by social pacts. At this stage, the prospective content of these pacts is fuzzy, but they will at least call for increased enforcement of existing social and environmental legislation, higher standards, and regular monitoring.

# NOTES

1. For the text of the president's statement, see Office of the Press Secretary, The White House, June 27, 1990.

2. Nellis Crigler and Stephen Lande, "Toward a Hemispheric Strategic Economic Alliance: Consideration by the Council of the Americas," Washington: Manchester Trade, February 14, 1990 (processed); and

"Trade Policy Proposals under the Enterprise for the Americas Initiative," Washington: Manchester Trade, August 20, 1990 (processed).

3. *Inside U.S. Trade*, October 5, 1990, 2.

4. Ibid.

5. *Inside U.S. Trade*, November 30, 1990, 3.

6. Statement by President Bush to the US Congress, Office of the Press Secretary, The White House, September 14, 1990.

7. For most Latin American countries, sharply higher oil prices in the wake of the Persian Gulf Crisis have curtailed the prospects for economic growth, at least through the first half of 1991. Mexico and Venezuela are big winners (perhaps together by $18 billion annually), but other countries are losers (Brazil by nearly $4 billion annually). See Stuart Tucker, "Big Winners and Many Losers Watch the Price of Oil," Overseas Development Council, November 20, 1990.

8. Data from UN Economic Commission for Latin America and the Caribbean, "Preliminary Overview of the Economy of Latin America and the Caribbean, 1990," Santiago, Chile, December 19, 1990.

9. The conditions and modalities of debt reduction are taken from the Office of the Press Secretary, The White House, September 14, 1990: "Enterprise for the Americas Initiative Act of 1990," HR 5855.

10. Richard E. Feinberg, Overseas Development Council, Testimony before the House of Representatives, Committee on Banking, Finance and Urban Affairs, Subcommittee on International Development, Finance, Trade and Monetary Policy, September 9, 1990.

11. These trade policies complemented domestic stabilization policies in the second half of the 1980s that sought to dampen inflationary pressures by cutting excessive government expenditures and to increase efficiency in production through privatization and deregulation. See John Williamson, *The Progress of Policy Reform in Latin America*, Institute for International Economics (Washington, January 1990), 24-26.

12. *Latin American Weekly Report*, September 20, 1990.

13. *The Wall Street Journal*, September 13, 1990, A16. See also *Financial Times*, September 6, 1990, 6 (wherein the Latin America Economic System expresses similar concerns).

14. See Feinberg, *op. cit.* During President Bush's five-nation trip to South America in early December 1990, the United States, Europe, and Japan cut off all new loans from the Inter-American Development Bank to Brazil until the Collor government makes significant progress with its commercial creditors. Brazil has not paid interest on its commercial debt in fifteen months and is now $8 billion in arrears (*New York Times*, December 5, 1990, A16).

15. The Latin American Integration Association (LAIA), formed by the Treaty of Montevideo in 1980, created an umbrella organization for the Andean Pact and the emerging group of Southern Cone countries. The LAIA members represent approximately 90 percent of Latin American population and gross national product, and about 80 percent of exports. The main countries outside LAIA are the Central American countries.

16. The figures cited here refer to import growth. For various reasons, export statistics for intra-group trade differ from import statistics. Correspondingly, trade growth stated in terms of export data would be different, but the picture of stagnation would remain much the same.

17. K. Khazeh and D. Clark, "A Case Study of Effects of Developing Country Integration on Trade Flows: The Andean Pact," *Journal of Latin American Studies* 22 (May 1990): 317-30.

18. The Quito Protocol of May 25, 1988, attempted to make Andean investment procedures and regional industrial programming more flexible. Progress was also made in lifting non-tariff barriers. The scope of the Quito Protocol, however, was nowhere near as ambitious as the La Paz Agreement of November 1990, discussed below.

19. *Journal of Commerce*, July 24, 1990, 11A.

20. Unclassified Cable 16915 from US Embassy La Paz, US State Department, December 3, 1990.

21. Nicaragua joined in 1956, giving the group nominal membership of the entire region except Panama and Belize.

22. Tim Coone and Rebecca Doulton, "Mexico Signs Central American Free-Trade Accord," *Financial Times*, January 15, 1991, 7.

23. CARICOM replaced the Caribbean Free Trade Association (CARIFTA), which was founded in 1965.

24. *Journal of Commerce,* June 5, 1990, 6B.

25. The rule of origin provision requires "substantial transformation" for goods made with foreign materials to qualify for free movement to other CARICOM countries.

26. For a detailed review of this meeting, see *Journal of Commerce,* December 4, 1990, 5A-7A. Updated information was obtained from the Eastern Caribbean Investment Promotion Service (ECIPS).

27. *Financial Times,* December 11, 1990, 14; *Wall Street Journal,* January 8, 1991, A10.

28. This section draws on: Jeffrey J. Schott, *United States-Canada Free Trade: An Evaluation of the Agreement,* Policy Analyses in International Economics 24, Institute for International Economics, April 1988; Jeffrey J. Schott and Murray G. Smith, *The Canada-United States Free Trade Agreement: The Global Impact,* Institute for International Economics, 1988.

29. The United States also has a free trade agreement with Israel, and a preferential trading arrangement with the Caribbean. But these agreements have a very small fraction of the economic impact of the US-Canada agreement.

30. Schott, *United States-Canada Free Trade,* 10-11.

31. The talks opened in May 1986; a draft agreement was initialed on October 3, 1987; the final text was completed on December 11, 1987; it was signed by President Reagan and Prime Minister Mulroney on January 2, 1988. Subsequently, after a bruising political battle in Canada, the FTA was ratified by each legislature and entered into force on January 1, 1989.

32. The figures in this paragraph are based on data provided by Sam Laird, International Economics Division, World Bank.

33. *Wall Street Journal,* November 28, 1990, A24.

34. John Williamson, *The Progress of Policy Reform in Latin America,* PA 28, Institute for International Economics, Table 10, January 1990.

35. Based on *Latin Finance* (December 1990): 36-37.

36. Gary Clyde Hufbauer, Jeffrey J. Schott and Kimberly Ann Elliott, *Economic Sanctions Reconsidered,* 2d ed., Institute for International Economics (1990).

37. Ronald J. Wonnacott, "U.S. Hub-and-Spoke Bilaterals and the Multilateral Trading System," C. D. Howe Institute, Commentary No. 23, October 1990.

38. *Inside U.S. Trade*, November 30, 1990, 3.

39. *Washington Post*, December 7, 1990, A53. Other official US statements single out Chile for talks right after Mexico. See *Wall Street Journal*, January 8, 1991, A10.

40. *Latin American Regional Report: Caribbean*, October 4, 1990.

41. The Lômé accords between the EC and former colonies in Africa, the Caribbean, and the Pacific might serve as a useful model. The Lômé accords established an institutional framework for regular public and private sector contacts on a wide variety of issues, including the environment, education, and infrastructure.

# Trade Is Not Enough

## Riordan Roett

To adequately understand the trade options and alternatives confronting the hemisphere in the 1990s, it is essential to first consider a set of corollary, but highly relevant, issues. The first category is that of the externalities over which Latin America and the Caribbean have little control, but will directly influence trade possibilities in this decade.

The first, and perhaps most pernicious from the hemisphere's perspective, is the emergence of world trading blocs. Inevitable or not (and I happen to believe they are), they stand to visibly influence Latin American economies. A North American Free Trade Area, a Yen-led bloc, and the European Community (EC) will face off in the 1990s with unknown implications for the world trading system. It is certain that Latin American and the Caribbean nations will feel the impact. Related to the "grouping" phenomenon is the probable failure—or at the very least, the lack of success—of the Uruguay Round of the current General Agreement on Tariffs and Trade (GATT) negotiations. The inability to reach a compromise on European agricultural subsidies will strongly influence the hemisphere's export possibilities in the years ahead.

As Wolf Grabendorff carefully illustrates in his essay, Europe does not give Latin America and the Caribbean a high priority. The focus of Europe is Europe: the consolidation of the EC and the emergence of Eastern European capitalism. If one examines the flow of direct foreign investment or the creation of trade openings, Latin America is a small and relatively marginal partner for Europe—pre or post-EC. Barbara Stallings's paper also clarifies the intentions of the Japanese in the hemisphere: she anticipates that the Japanese will approach Latin America (with the exception of Mexico) on a limited basis and very slowly given the emergence of a North American Free Trade Area. Thus, the European and Yen-led trade or investment groupings, sometimes cited as alternatives to the United States, do not appear anxious, or likely, to play a significant role in the years ahead. They will both be present; current investment will be maintained; selective new investments will be made; but the message of the Grabendorff and Stallings essays is clear: the United States will remain the "best hope" for the countries of Latin America and the Caribbean for trade and investment options.

## Impediments to Enhanced Trade

The overhang of Latin American and Caribbean debt continues to plague the region. The 1989 Brady Plan for debt reduction is underfunded and will remain so in a world growing short of capital. The flow of private commercial bank loans has all but ceased, and the "officialization" of the debt is a new phenomenon. In 1982, less than 40 percent of the Third World debt was held by official creditors; in 1990, it surpassed 50 percent. That means that the private commercial banks have begun to exit from Latin American debt through a variety of debt reduction schemes. The official lending institutions and the governments of the industrial countries are now the majority holders of the debt incurred in the 1970s and 1980s.

It is now recognized (albeit belatedly) that the international debt management policy of the 1980s did not work. The assumption that an expanding world economy would act as an engine of growth for Latin America was incorrect. Latin America did not take part in the expansion because the growth of world trade favored the exporters of manufactured goods rather than those who exported primary goods. It favored those countries with the capital and technology needed to modernize production processes quickly in order to take advantage of new market opportunities—as the Asian countries did so with great success. The countries of this hemisphere did not—or were unable to do so.

Oil exporters in Latin America and the Caribbean (as elsewhere in the Third World) were adversely affected in the 1980s by low petroleum prices. Other commodity export prices lost ground, also. The terms of trade of the region declined by more than 20 percent in the 1980s. An additional burden was that interest rates remained high throughout most of the decade. Since the bulk of the Latin American debt had been incurred under variable interest rates, high rates meant an additional outgoing flow of capital.

The interest and dividend payments of the region exceeded the new capital received by more than $200 billion in the 1980s. The countries of the hemisphere were capital exporters at a moment in their development when they should have been capital importers. Current prospects are for a further increase in Third World debt in 1990-91, despite the various initiatives to lower the debt burden.

The linkage between trade and debt, then, is obvious. The countries of the region generated large export surpluses in the 1980s to earn the foreign exchange required to service the debt. They also drastically cut imports with a sharp negative impact on their previous suppliers, especially the United States. As the Latin American countries confront a potentially more hostile world trade situation—caused by the collapse of the Uruguay Round and related matters—they face continued debt-servicing obligations (although only five countries—Chile, Colombia, El Salvador, Mexico, and Uruguay—were not in arrears by the end of 1990).

Thus, it is critical to understand that trade is the "reverse side" of debt. As long as the Brady Plan is underfunded and there is little possibility of "official" relief through the Paris Club or an alternative arrangement, the impasse will continue. Latin America will be hard pressed to generate trade surpluses to service existing debt (and cut back sharply on imports). To the degree that the world environment—trade blocs, no GATT agreement—makes that difficult, we will fail to find a solution for the trade-debt conundrum.

The issue is further complicated by the "third leg" of growth. In addition to the need to export and the obligation to service outstanding debt obligations, direct foreign investment becomes a critical factor in renewing growth in the region. In the absence of new private commercial bank loans and the imbalance in the flow of capital—Latin America and the Caribbean exporting rather than importing capital—a critical variable will be new direct foreign investment. Given the low level of interest on the part of Europe and Japan, US investors will be critical, but US and foreign investors both remain concerned with the debt overhang that precludes Latin American governments from investing in infrastructure, technology, and research and development. Investors are also wary of the impending trade blocs and the degree to which a manufacturing or production base in Latin America will prejudice worldwide patterns of sources and multinational marketing strategies.

One of the ironies confronting Latin America is that almost all of the governments of the region are now undertaking the fundamental reforms urged on them in the 1960s and 1970s. Though fiercely resistant during those two decades to such reforms, changes in leadership and form of regime and rapidly evolving international economic realities have convinced the current governments to undertake fiscal and tax reform, financial liberalization, privatization, deregulation, an opening to direct foreign investment, and related policy initiatives. The expectation of decisionmakers in the region was that their willingness to adopt a broad program of reform would bring benefits, either in trade opportunities and/or in further support for debt reduction schemes, and/or new foreign direct investment.

Unfortunately, the story has been otherwise. Former military regimes have been replaced with civilian, democratic governments, but without the sort of policy support they expected—and deserved from the international community. Regimes that have been civilian for some years, such as Venezuela, have adopted rigorous reform policies, but have received little preferential treatment in recognition of the political and social difficulties involved in such reform. A number of countries experienced delicate and difficult transitions to democracy after years of repressive military government. Heightened social expectations on the part of their populations have gone unmet given the difficulty of meeting international obligations and the realities of the new interdependent global system with which they must cope.

Hufbauer and Schott mention, as one of the five preconditions for a free trade arrangement in the hemisphere, the need for the existence of a "functioning democracy." As they correctly state, "a trade agreement with a dictatorship will often be at risk of interruption by the United States." Given the widespread existence of democratic regimes, now is the time to move to consolidate that "precondition" with reasonable policies on trade, debt, and investment policy.

The other preconditions set forth by Hufbauer and Schott—a reasonable degree of monetary stability, a willingness to accept the tenets of a market economy and reject the teachings of statism, an ability and willingness of the government to look to other revenue sources than imposts on international transactions, and trade linkage—have begun to assert themselves in the hemisphere. Thus, the "preconditions," perhaps for the first time in this century, are or will be present.

Given the externalities discussed above, and the impasse over trade and debt strategies, a new hemispheric trade order will need to reconsider the three strands of development emphasized in the Bush initiative: debt, trade, and investment.

The Brady Plan will need to be "beefed-up" with further enhancements from the public sector. Increased recognition, through more opportunities for debt reduction, will be needed for those governments continuing with structural reform programs. On the trade side, Peter Drucker, a leading management consultant, has persuasively argued that the answer to the US trade deficit is not continued confrontation with Japan; it is reopening Latin American markets for US exports. Drucker's argument is persuasive if one examines the nature of the trade patterns between North and South America and examines the trade opportunities lost to American firms since Latin America was forced to drastically curtail imports—primarily those from the United States.

The trade relationship explains why the United States and the Cairns Group, which contains the principal Latin American agricultural exporters, are united in their position at the GATT talks with regard to eliminating EC agricultural subsidies. Both will stand to benefit if trade is liberalized. Both will be hurt if it is not.

Finally, direct foreign investment will seek the best profit opportunity. To the degree that Latin America is burdened with debt, and trade possibilities are limited, investors will continue to look on Europe and Asia as more attractive. It is critical that the US policymaking community understand the tight relationship between trade, debt, and investment. Given the new climate in Latin America and the Caribbean—governments committed to modernization and reform—it is critical that these regimes receive a modicum of support. The new hemispheric trade order, then, will depend on trade options; but it will also be nourished or starved to the degree that debt relief—not forgiveness—is postponed or overlooked and to the degree to which the direct foreign investor downgrades Latin America as a logical investment site.

Having lost out in the expansion of the world economy in the 1980s, the Latin American and Caribbean states cannot afford to do so again in the 1990s, especially if there is another mid-decade expansion. They need to prepare now. An important element in that preparation is the need to invest in productivity and to become increasingly competitive. The only way they will find the funds to do so is to decrease the outward flow of capital and to find increased "space" in the international system for their products. The degree to which the global system turns against Latin America and the Caribbean, and other Third World countries committed to reform, will increase the possibility for a long impasse in trade and investment relations between the developed and developing countries. A judicious commitment to supporting institutional change in Latin America and the Caribbean now, through debt reduction and increased trade opportunities, should facilitate new investment flows by mid-decade and further enhance the emergence of a modern and competitive trade regime later in the 1990s.

# 2

# The Single European Market and Its Impact on US-Latin American Trade Relations

## Wolf Grabendorff*

The imminent completion of the Single European Market (SEM) has produced a great deal of anxiety among the European Community's (EC) trading partners, developed and developing alike. Given the recent dynamics of the EC's economic development and its 38 percent participation in world trade—excluding intra-EC trade, which makes up about 60 percent of the member states' foreign trade, EC participation still accounts for 20 percent of all world trade—it is not surprising that the possible effects of the SEM are widely discussed, even more so after the breakdown of the General Agreement on Tariffs and Trade (GATT) negotiations.

In addition to inter-regional trade relations, the implementation of the SEM will affect many other areas of international economic relations. In this respect, this chapter will first briefly discuss some major features and trends of EC-Latin American economic relations. Section two then will consider the SEM's effects on world trade, specifically with regard to its impact on third countries. Also, in section two, this chapter will examine in greater detail what those effects might be for developing countries. Section three will single out the possible effects the SEM will have on Latin American trade relations with the EC, as analyzed in a hitherto unpublished study by the *Instituto de Relaciones Europeo-Latinoamericanas* (IRELA). Lastly, based on the possible scenarios for Latin American-EC trade relations after 1992, sections four and five will address the possible impact of such developments on US-Latin American trade relations and draw some cautious conclusions on possible outlooks for the immediate future.

*Special thanks to Stefano Mainardi for his research assistance.

## Recent Features and Tendencies of EC-Latin American Relations

From a Latin American perspective, relations with the EC are seen in light of the continuous decline of the trade relationship. Criticism centers upon the protectionism resulting from the EC's Common Agricultural Policy (CAP) and the subsidized export of its agricultural surplus.

This view, which came to the fore during the difficult negotiations of the Uruguay Round, tends to overlook the important elements of EC-Latin American economic relations with regard to the increase of Official Development Assistance (ODA) and the new instruments developed by the EC with regard to furthering the industrial cooperation between the two regions. While some of these instruments will indirectly aid the process of restructuring the trade relationship between the two regions over the long term, one has to acknowledge that, in spite of all the EC initiatives, the problems in the economic relationship between the two regions will remain for years to come.[1]

The EC's ODA represents nearly 6 percent of its total budget expenditures. Compared to bilateral aid of its member countries, ODA appears more concentrated towards EC-associated African countries: almost 60 percent of this assistance is provided to these countries, while EC member states' bilateral aid to the same region constitutes only 45 percent of the total. Moreover, among nonassociated developing countries, more EC aid is channeled to Asia than to Latin America, since the latter region absorbs only one-third of the development assistance granted to this group of countries.

In the period 1987-89, ODA to Latin America from the EC and from its eight member states belonging to the Organisation for Economic Cooperation and Development (OECD) Development Aid Committee (DAC), excluding Ireland and including Spain, represented about 47 percent of DAC's total ODA. The eight member states are Belgium, Denmark, Germany, France, Holland, Italy, Spain, and the United Kingdom. The EC's share of this contribution was just 19 percent, while the eight member states accounted for the remaining 81 percent (Table 1). Yet, the EC's contribution, including a high grant component, is counterbalanced by a strong orientation towards projects in the social sector, particularly the rural areas. Financial and technical assistance, followed by food aid, comprise nearly 50 percent of the EC's ODA (Table 2). The

## Table 1. Origin of Bilateral Official Development Aid Received by Latin America, 1985-89

(net payments in millions of dollars; share of total aid provided by DAC countries to Latin America; annual increase)

| | 1985 | | | 1986 | | | 1987 | | | 1988 | | | 1989 | | |
|---|---|---|---|---|---|---|---|---|---|---|---|---|---|---|---|
| | Value | Part. % | Incr. % | Value | Part. % | Incr. % | Value | Part. % | Incr. % | Value | Part. % | Incr. % | Value | Part. % | Incr. % |
| Belgium | 12.0 | 0.6 | -23.4 | 18.0 | 0.8 | 47.1 | 22.6 | 0.8 | 25.6 | 25.6 | 1.0 | 13.3 | 21.1 | 0.7 | -17.6 |
| Denmark | 6.0 | 0.2 | 119.2 | 4.0 | 0.1 | -31.6 | 14.0 | 0.5 | 250.0 | 14.6 | 0.6 | 4.3 | 11.0 | 0.4 | -24.7 |
| Spain | n.a | n.a | n.a | n.a | n.a | n.a | 31.5 | 1.2 | - | 64.8 | 2.5 | 105.7 | 57.0ᵃ | 2.0 | -12.0 |
| France | 101.0 | 5.0 | 20.0 | 174.0 | 7.8 | 71.1 | 171.3 | 6.3 | -1.6 | 132.8 | 5.1 | -22.5 | 112.9 | 4.0 | -15.0 |
| Netherlands | 82.0 | 4.0 | -16.5 | 94.0 | 4.1 | 14.1 | 124.0 | 4.6 | 31.9 | 150.3 | 5.7 | 21.2 | 167.9 | 5.9 | 11.7 |
| Italy | 67.0 | 3.2 | 49.7 | 108.0 | 4.8 | 61.1 | 130.8 | 4.8 | 21.1 | 248.1 | 9.5 | 89.7 | 404.9 | 14.3 | 63.2 |
| FRG | 196.0 | 9.8 | 11.1 | 315.0 | 14.0 | 60.5 | 471.9 | 17.3 | 49.8 | 364.7 | 13.9 | -22.7 | 360.1 | 12.8 | -1.3 |
| United Kingdom | 13.0 | 0.6 | -7.1 | 14.0 | 0.6 | 3.8 | 14.0 | 0.5 | 0.0 | 23.5 | 0.9 | 67.9 | 25.3 | 0.9 | 7.7 |
| Total 8 | 477.0 | 23.7 | 9.1 | 727.0 | 32.4 | 51.9 | 980.1 | 36.0 | 34.8 | 1024.4 | 39.2 | 4.5 | 1160.2 | 41.1 | 13.3 |
| EC | 104.0 | 5.2 | 7.2 | 148.0 | 6.6 | 42.3 | 173.9 | 6.4 | 17.5 | 281.2 | 10.8 | 61.7 | 245.6 | 8.7 | -12.7 |
| Total EC 8 countries | 581.0 | 28.9 | 8.8 | 875.0 | 39.1 | 50.6 | 1154.0 | 42.4 | 31.9 | 1305.6 | 49.9 | 13.1 | 1405.8 | 49.8 | 7.7 |
| US | 1204.0 | 60.0 | 30.9 | 1048.0 | 46.9 | -13.0 | 1164.0 | 42.8 | 11.1 | 1002.0 | 38.3 | -13.9 | 899.0 | 31.8 | -10.3 |
| Japan | 194.0 | 9.6 | -6.8 | 300.0 | 13.4 | 54.9 | 412.0 | 15.1 | 37.3 | 386.9 | 14.8 | -6.1 | 529.2 | 18.7 | 36.8 |
| Total DACᵇ | 2012.0 | 100.0 | 17.3 | 2236.0 | 100.0 | 11.1 | 2720.3 | 100.0 | 21.7 | 2615.2 | 100.0 | -3.9 | 2822.8 | 100.0 | 7.9 |

ᵃPreliminary estimate.
ᵇThe member countries of the Development Aid Committee (DAC) of the OECD are Australia, Austria, Belgium, Canada, Denmark, Finland, France, Italy, Japan, the Netherlands, Ireland, New Zealand, Norway, Sweden, Switzerland, the United Kingdom, the United States, and the Federal Republic of Germany.

Source: Calculated on the basis of OECD data. Ministerio de Economía y Hacienda: Información Comercial Española, Boletín ICE Económico, Madrid, 1988, 1989, 1990.

## Table 2. EC Cooperation with Latin America, 1989

(millions of ECUs)

Development Cooperation

| BUDGETARY ITEMS | 9310, 9313 Financial Technical Aid | 937 Stabex | 941 NGOs | D920 951 Food Aid | Subtotal |
|---|---|---|---|---|---|
| Costa Rica | 0.6 | - | 0.1 | - | 0.8 |
| El Salvador | - | - | 0.8 | 0.3 | 1.1 |
| Guatemala | - | - | 1 | 1.2 | 2.2 |
| Honduras | - | - | 0.4 | 2.4 | 2.8 |
| Nicaragua | - | - | 4.7 | 11.2 | 16 |
| Panama | - | - | 0.1 | - | 0.1 |
| REGIONAL ACTIONS | 49.5 | - | - | - | 49.5 |
| TOTAL CENTRAL AMERICA | 50.1 | - | 7.2 | 15 | 74.4 |
| Bolivia | 18.6 | - | 1.7 | 9 | 29.2 |
| Colombia | - | - | 1.3 | 0.2 | 1.5 |
| Ecuador | 0.3 | - | 0.4 | 2.6 | 3.3 |
| Peru | 1.2 | - | 1.9 | 9.5 | 12.6 |
| Venezuela | - | - | 0.5 | - | 0.5 |
| REGIONAL ACTIONS | 11.2 | - | - | - | 11.2 |
| TOTAL ANDEAN PACT | 31.1 | - | 5.6 | 21.3 | 58.2 |
| Argentina | - | - | 0.8 | - | 0.8 |
| Brazil | - | - | 2.9 | 9.7 | 12.7 |
| Chile | - | - | 2.9 | 3.5 | 6.4 |
| Paraguay | - | - | 0.4 | 1.5 | 1.9 |
| Uruguay | - | - | 0.4 | 0.2 | 0.6 |
| TOTAL SOUTHERN CONE | - | - | 7.4 | 14.9 | 22.3 |
| Cuba | - | - | 0.02 | 4 | 4 |
| Haiti | 5.5 | 5.9 | 0.7 | 5.8 | 17.9 |
| Mexico | 3.1 | - | 0.6 | 0.1 | 3.8 |
| Dominican Repub. | - | - | 0.2 | 0.4 | 0.6 |
| REGIONAL ACTIONS LATIN AMERICA | 1.9 | - | - | - | 1.9 |
| OVERALL TOTAL | 91.9 | 5.9 | 21.8 | 61.5 | 181.1 |

(continued)

## Table 2. (Continued) EC Cooperation with Latin America, 1989

(millions of ECUs)

Humanitarian Aid

| BUDGETARY ITEMS | 936 Refug. | 944 Evalua. Food aid | 949 Fight drugs | 950 Emerg. aid | 954 Fight AIDS | Subtotal |
|---|---|---|---|---|---|---|
| Costa Rica | - | - | - | - | - | - |
| El Salvador | 1.5 | - | - | 2 | - | 3.5 |
| Guatemala | 3.3 | - | - | - | 0.02 | 3.3 |
| Honduras | - | - | - | - | 0.2 | 0.2 |
| Nicaragua | 1.5 | 0.01 | - | - | 0.3 | 1.8 |
| Panama | - | - | - | - | - | - |
| REGIONAL ACTIONS | - | - | - | - | - | - |
| TOTAL CENTRAL AMERICA | 6.3 | 0.01 | - | 2 | 0.47 | 8.8 |
| Bolivia | - | - | - | - | 0.2 | 0.2 |
| Colombia | - | - | - | - | - | - |
| Ecuador | - | - | - | - | - | - |
| Peru | - | - | - | - | 0.2 | 0.2 |
| Venezuela | - | - | - | 0.5 | - | 0.5 |
| REGIONAL ACTIONS | - | - | - | - | - | - |
| TOTAL ANDEAN PACT | - | - | - | 0.5 | 0.4 | 0.9 |
| Argentina | - | - | - | 0.4 | - | 0.4 |
| Brazil | - | - | - | - | 0.1 | 0.1 |
| Chile | 0.7 | - | - | - | - | 0.7 |
| Paraguay | - | - | - | - | - | - |
| Uruguay | - | - | - | - | - | - |
| TOTAL SOUTHERN CONE | 0.7 | - | - | 0.4 | 0.1 | 1.2 |
| Cuba | - | - | - | - | - | - |
| Haiti | - | - | - | - | - | - |
| Mexico | 3 | - | 0.4 | - | 0.2 | 3.5 |
| Dominican Republic | - | - | - | - | 0.4 | 0.4 |
| REGIONAL ACTIONS LATIN AMERICA | 0.04 | - | - | - | - | 0.01 |
| OVERALL TOTAL | 10 | 0.01 | 0.4 | 2.9 | 1.5 | 14.8 |

(continued)

## Table 2. (Continued) EC Cooperation with Latin America, 1989

(millions of ECUs)

Economic Cooperation

| BUGETARY ITEMS | 706 Energ. Program | 707 Energ. Polic. | 7330 7309 Scien. Coop. | 9311 9315 Trade Promo. | 9312 Reg. Integ. | 9314 9281 Train. | 946 Envir. | 990 Trade Econo. Coop. | Sub-total | TOT. |
|---|---|---|---|---|---|---|---|---|---|---|
| Costa Rica | - | - | 0.2 | 0.3 | - | - | - | - | 0.4 | 1.2 |
| El Salvador | - | - | - | - | - | - | - | - | - | 4.6 |
| Guatemala | - | - | 0.2 | - | - | - | - | - | 0.2 | 5.7 |
| Honduras | - | - | - | - | - | - | - | - | - | 3 |
| Nicaragua | - | - | 0.1 | 0.2 | 0.1 | - | - | - | 0.4 | 18.1 |
| Panama | - | - | 0.03 | - | - | - | - | - | 0.3 | 0.2 |
| REGIONAL ACTIONS | - | - | - | 0.9 | - | - | - | 0.1 | 1 | 50.5 |
| TOTAL CENTRAL AMERICA | - | - | 0.45 | 1.4 | 0.1 | - | - | 0.1 | 2.12 | 83.3 |
| Bolivia | - | - | 0.01 | - | - | - | - | - | 0.01 | 29.4 |
| Colombia | - | - | 0.6 | 0.1 | - | - | 0.3 | - | 1.1 | 2.6 |
| Ecuador | - | - | - | - | - | - | 0.2 | - | 0.2 | 3.4 |
| Peru | 0.3 | - | - | 1.8 | - | 0.4 | - | - | 2.4 | 15.2 |
| Venezuela | - | - | 0.1 | - | - | - | - | - | 0.1 | 1 |
| REGIONAL ACTIONS | - | - | 0.1 | - | 0.1 | 0.7 | - | 4.6 | 5.5 | 16.7 |
| TOTAL ANDEAN PACT | 0.3 | - | 0.8 | 1.9 | 0.1 | 1.1 | 0.5 | 4.6 | 9.25 | 68.3 |
| Argentina | 0.2 | 0.4 | 0.2 | 0.9 | - | - | - | - | 1.3 | 2.5 |
| Brasil | 0.3 | - | 1.1 | - | 0.3 | 0.2 | - | 0.4 | 2.3 | 15 |
| Chile | - | - | - | - | - | 0.04 | - | - | 0.04 | 7.1 |
| Paraguay | - | - | - | 0.2 | - | 0.03 | - | - | 0.21 | 2.1 |
| Uruguay | - | - | - | 0.2 | - | - | 0.02 | 0.1 | 0.3 | 0.9 |
| TOTAL SOUTHERN CONE | 0.4 | 0.04 | 1.3 | 1.3 | 0.3 | 0.24 | 0.02 | 0.5 | 4.1 | 27.7 |
| Cuba | - | - | - | - | - | - | - | - | - | 4 |
| Haiti | - | - | - | - | - | - | - | - | - | 17.9 |
| Mexico | 0.3 | 0.2 | 1.2 | 0.1 | - | - | - | 0.1 | 1.9 | 9.3 |
| Dominican Republic | - | - | - | - | - | - | - | - | 0.01 | 1 |
| REGIONAL ACTIONS LATIN AMERICA | 0.4 | - | - | - | 0.9 | 2.5 | 0.2 | 1 | 9.7 | 11.6 |
| OVERALL TOTAL | 1.4 | 0.2 | 3.7 | 9.4 | 1.5 | 3.8 | 0.7 | 6.3 | 27.1 | 223 |

Source: Calculated on the basis of EC Commission data.

poorer countries in Central America and the Andean region are the principal beneficiaries of this assistance.

According to the new guidelines of the EC commission relating to development cooperation with nonassociated countries,[2] the EC's development assistance to Latin America should be geared to the recipient country's level of economic progress. In fact, the guidelines draw a further distinction between less developed economies, for which the traditional tools of financial and technical cooperation should continue to play a major role, and other relatively more advanced economies that need other kinds of assistance, such as foreign investment promotion for joint production programs and cooperation in science and technology.

In 1989-90, various initiatives were promoted to support and strengthen the increasingly selective use of development cooperation. In 1988, new programs for industrial cooperation between the two regions were established. These programs were efficiently geared to identify the needs of recipient countries, to contribute to the transfer of know-how and technology, and to aid in the progressive opening of their economies, while stimulating integrated production and marketing activities of enterprises in both Central America and the Andean region. These new programs envisage the supply of financial assistance to promote joint ventures between small and medium-sized European companies and local enterprises ("EC International Investment Partners") and the extension of a computerized network of European enterprises to Latin American countries (BC-NET).

Furthermore, the EC has granted specific support to the countries most affected by illicit drug production. The EC has agreed to remove, for the next four years, its tariff barriers to exports from Bolivia, Colombia, Ecuador, and Peru, which thus receive the same treatment as the least developed countries within the Generalized System of Preferences (GSP). This measure is intended to stimulate alternative crops production.

On the whole, more attention is paid to the support of private-sector initiatives and local entrepreneurs' associations, environmental and demographic problems, and local food production. This interest corresponds to the overall tendency of the EC's development cooperation, as seen, for instance, in the renewal of the Lômé Convention (Lômé IV) by the greater emphasis on these issues and the inclusion of specific new sections for other issues. Furthermore, the process of democratization and the deepening of regional integration pursued by Latin American countries have received support from the EC, which considers them as a means for achieving closer ties between the two regions. In this respect, the EC has provided remarkable technical and financial assistance to foster initiatives of economic cooperation in several subregions, such as in Central America and the Southern Cone.

Concerning investment flows, in contrast to the stagnation of trade flows, as examined in section three, the EC has demonstrated an active involvement over the last decade in Latin America by strengthening its presence relative to the United States, especially in Brazil, Argentina, and the countries of the Andean Pact. In the late 1970s, the major EC investor countries accounted for about one-fourth of total direct investment from the EC, the United States, and Japan. A decade later, the EC members' contribution amounted to more than 45 percent, in spite of a significant increase in the investment outflows from the other two major investor countries (Table 3). Chile draws the highest relative advantage from foreign direct investment as measured by its percentage of gross domestic product (GDP), which averaged more than 5 percent in 1987-89 and was estimated at 6 percent in 1989.[3]

**Table 3. Direct Investments by EC Member Countries, the US, and Japan in Latin America,[a] 1977-88**

(millions of dollars)

| Country of origin | 1977-78 | 1979-80 | 1981-82 | 1983-84 | 1985-86 | 1987-88 |
|---|---|---|---|---|---|---|
| Belgium | -9.3 | 60.7 | 30.1 | 31.0 | 21.3 | 244.0 |
| Denmark | n.a. | n.a. | 6.8 | - | - | - |
| Spain | 209.5 | 379.5 | 458.9 | 170.1 | 175.1 | 383.5 |
| France | 257.6 | 432.8 | 720.6 | 221.3 | 227.5 | 205.0 |
| Italy | -25.0 | 388.3 | -67.5 | 342.5 | 129.6 | 288.0 |
| Netherlands | 110.2 | 142.0 | 216.6 | 185.7 | 180.2 | 154.0 |
| United Kingdom | 444.6 | 535.0 | 664.0 | 672.8 | 1574.8 | 1889.0 |
| West Germany | 543.6 | 695.8 | 772.1 | 582.1 | 137.2 | 790.0 |
| TOTAL EC | 1531.2 | 2634.1 | 2801.6 | 2205.5 | 2445.7 | 3953.5 |
| US | 4505.0 | 5642.0 | 4678.0 | -210.0 | 523.0 | 2144.0 |
| Japan[b] | 628.4 | 1354.6 | 1948.1 | 2360.1 | 2543.5 | 2390.0 |

[a]Latin America comprises: South America, Central America, Mexico, Panama, Cuba, Haiti, Jamaica, the Dominican Republic, and Trinidad and Tobago.
[b]As of 1981, Japanese investments were concentrated in Panama.

A few studies have pointed out different features of European versus US or Japanese multinational companies operating in Latin America with regard to aspects like product diversification, technology adaptation, and linkages with local suppliers.[4] On the whole, the results are neither homogeneous nor consistent, and can be partially explained by the different sectoral distributions of the samples used for these analyses.

The ongoing policies of structural adjustment and the progressive opening of Latin American economies can contribute to attract new inflows of foreign investment from both US and European enterprises, while the latter could be further stimulated by the SEM's implementation.

## The SEM and Its Implications for World Trade

The different mechanisms that, for the most part, allow for the free movement of goods, services, capital, and persons among the twelve member states of the EC after 1992 are mainly concerned with intra-EC regulations that facilitate a high degree of competition between European or European-based enterprises. The possible effects of harmonization efforts on foreign trade can be characterized in two ways:

- Increased international competitiveness of European enterprises will give rise to the possibility of easing previously existing trade barriers, assuming that third countries will reciprocate—with exceptions in the case of developing countries.[5]
- Increased internal competitiveness might give rise to calls for the postponement of trade liberalization measures, given the need for intra-EC enterprises to adapt internally to the new realities of the SEM.

The ways in which such apparently contradictory effects are played out will depend on economic pressure groups and the member states' awareness of the winners and losers in the process of completing the SEM. It is, therefore, difficult to foresee the extent to which increased competitiveness within the EC will be beneficial for the liberalization of the trade regime with third countries—an effect that is certainly intended by the EC authorities, and that found expression during the negotiations of the Uruguay Round.

Given the importance of the CAP for the general integration effect and consensus-building within the EC, it was not surprising that the successful conclusion of the Uruguay Round has been held up by CAP-related issues. The EC is the world's largest importer and the second largest exporter (not including intra-EC trade) of agricultural products, and, therefore, is sensitive to changes in the agricultural trade structure—although such changes are, without doubt, necessary. The effects of the CAP on the international economy are distorting, not only with regard to excessive production, but also to price support for exports to third countries; such effects are especially negative with regard to some Latin American countries.[6] It can generally be assumed that the effects of the SEM on the CAP will be somewhat limited, since all possible changes with regard to the trade-related issues of CAP will have to come from GATT agreements.

The position of developing countries relative to this issue is far from unanimous. Whereas most of these countries endeavour to secure easier access to industrial countries for their agricultural exports, a complete and rapid implementation of agricultural trade liberalization by the major world producers would probably result in higher food import prices for countries dependent on imports of cereals, meat, and dairy products. In Latin America, the benefits of such a liberalization process would be concentrated in only a few countries, while short to medium-term costs would be spread over several countries in the region. In the short run, significant benefits are estimated to accrue to Argentina, Brazil, and Cuba, even if Brazil is also a strong importer of the temperate agricultural products mentioned above. The net income effect, however, would still be positive for the region as a whole.[7]

As far as industrial products are concerned, given their relatively higher income elasticity and price elasticity of demand, they are more likely to be affected by the incremental growth effects and the regulatory changes brought about by the SEM. Among these products, some highly research and development intensive goods (e.g., telecommunications materials) will possibly overcome present diseconomies of scale through the elimination of intra-EC barriers. The corresponding import flows to the EC market might consequently undergo some trade diversion, while EC exports could be strengthened.

This result may reverse or at least change the negative trend of the 1970s and 1980s, when production of the manufacturing sector grew much more slowly in the EC than in the United States and Japan. Between 1973 and 1985 the corresponding EC growth rate was, respectively, six and eight times lower than the US and Japanese rates. This slow performance, contrasted with the comparatively high growth of internal demand in the EC, particularly for high-tech goods, was offset by the increasing contribution of imports.[8]

Common EC-wide trade and industrial policy measures will have to substitute for national barriers applied by individual member states for "sensitive" products (e.g., textiles, cars, iron, and steel). At present, these products are subject to quotas and other trade restrictions. The outcome will depend on the nature of the compromise between those member states that are more liberal and open, and those that are the more protectionist. The EC has used quotas and voluntary export restraint agreements to protect its markets to a lesser extent from Latin American countries than from other regions, particularly Asia and Eastern Europe. Hence the eventual removal or "downward" harmonization of such measures at the EC level should benefit Latin America, albeit to a more limited degree.

As previously mentioned, the increased international competitiveness of European industry is likely to affect the developing countries' exports to some extent. Nevertheless, recent trends in the EC's external trade policy, as in the case of the renewal of the GSP, point to an increased differentiation in the preferential access granted to developing countries, thus hindering such access for the relatively more competitive exporters.[9] The efforts at granting a differentiated preferential treatment to the poorer economies is, in any case, partly justified by the particularly low use that these countries have made so far of the GSP.

## The Possible Effects of the SEM on Latin America

Latin American trade relations with the EC are characterized by asymmetry, and by the relatively marginal role of Latin America in the EC's foreign trade, which can be explained in three very basic ways:

- Unlike other areas of the developing world, such as the African, Caribbean, and Pacific states and the Mediterranean countries, Latin America does not benefit from specific EC policies of preferences, except for the GSP, which applies to all developing countries.
- About three-quarters of Latin American exports to the EC are primary products, for which a relatively lower demand elasticity exists; this has often been coupled with a high degree of substitution during the last decade, and exacerbated by the CAP policies.

• Latin American exports to the EC lack diversification, especially with regard to semimanufactured or manufactured goods.

Nevertheless, Latin American exports to the EC have increased by some 6 percent from 1988 to 1989, reaching $29 billion (Table 4). From 1980 to 1988 the average annual increase was only around 2 percent. Although the participation of imports from Latin America in overall EC imports decreased from more than 7 percent in 1985 to 5.9 percent in 1989, EC exports to Latin America increased by almost 7 percent between 1988 and 1989, reaching more than $17 billion. This left Latin America with a positive trade balance of $11.9 billion in 1989.[10]

The asymmetrical nature of the EC-Latin American trade relations has been structural for decades. While the EC mainly exports industrial goods, Latin America trades agricultural and other primary products.

### Table 4. EC Trade with Latin America-20,[*] 1965-89

(millions of dollars)

| Year | EC-12 Imports | | Balance | EC-12 Exports | |
|------|-------|-----------------|---------|-------|------------------|
|      | Value | Growth Y.rate(%) |         | Value | Growth Y.rate (%) |
| 1965 | 3,801  | -     | 1,529  | 2,272  | -     |
| 1970 | 4,967  | -     | 1,090  | 3,877  | -     |
| 1975 | 9,683  | -     | -717   | 10,400 | -     |
| 1980 | 23,160 | 24.6  | 4,074  | 19,086 | 15.9  |
| 1981 | 22,843 | -1.4  | 4,008  | 18,835 | -1.3  |
| 1982 | 21,549 | -5.7  | 6,630  | 14,919 | -20.8 |
| 1983 | 22,180 | 2.9   | 10,765 | 11,415 | -23.5 |
| 1984 | 22,875 | 3.1   | 10,990 | 11,885 | 4.1   |
| 1985 | 23,104 | 1.0   | 11,232 | 11,872 | -0.1  |
| 1986 | 20,018 | -13.4 | 5,731  | 14,287 | 20.3  |
| 1987 | 22,508 | 12.4  | 6,557  | 15,951 | 11.6  |
| 1988 | 27,437 | 21.9  | 11,230 | 16,207 | 1.6   |
| 1989 | 29,175 | 6.3   | 11,882 | 17,293 | 6.7   |

[*]Latin America-20 = Mexico, Guatemala, Honduras, El Salvador, Nicaragua, Costa Rica, Panama, Cuba, Haiti, Dominican Republic, Colombia, Venezuela, Ecuador, Peru, Brazil, Chile, Bolivia, Paraguay, Uruguay, and Argentina.

Source: Commission of the European Communities.

Latin America, therefore, suffers greatly from the price fluctuations of primary products, as well as their increased production or substitution by the EC. In contrast with the experience of the newly industrializing Asian countries, Latin American countries have so far failed to sufficiently diversify their exports to the EC. This negative performance can probably be attributed more to their lack of quality standards than to EC import barriers restricting the access of these products in the European market.

At present, nearly two-thirds of total Latin American exports outside the region consist of primary products. Compared to the corresponding figure for 1980, there has been a decrease of more than 15 percent in the region's total export share of these products. Changes in volumes and the negative trend in primary product prices are partly responsible for the reduction. With regard to volume, the saturation of the outlet markets in industrial countries has meant that tropical products for export have undergone slow growth, and this has been a major problem for some Central American and Caribbean economies. Secondly, for certain products, there has been a substitution of temperate products for tropical ones (e.g., vegetable oil versus coconut oil), or a reduction in the consumption of energy-intensive products for industrial use (e.g., copper) and of natural resources for agricultural use.

World commodity prices have been adversely affected by two things. First, the price trend has been influenced by the substantial increase in international interest rates, which has inflated the costs of storage and buffer stocks of primary products and the debt service of debtor countries, thus forcing currency devaluations and efforts to increase exports by these countries. Second, prices are affected by the stronger fluctuations in the exchange rates—which have restored pressures for a new protectionism—and the overvaluation of the US dollar, which has obliged primary producers using dollars (such as Latin American producers) to reduce their sale prices in order to remain competitive in countries whose currencies have been losing value relative to the US dollar.[11] On the other hand, the devaluation of the US dollar since 1986 and the policies of internal demand control implemented in the United States have more recently impeded the maintenance by Latin American countries of a high trade surplus with the United States.

In the case of EC-Latin American trade relations, the share of food and primary products, including fuel, fluctuated during the 1980s between 60 and 80 percent of Latin America's total commodity exports to the EC

(Table 5). As with trade relations with other developed regions, this sectoral bias towards primary products seems diluted by a gradual diversification in composition according to product: the thirteen main Latin American commodities exported to the EC accounted for 83 percent of the total in 1985, and 73 percent in 1988.[12]

Nevertheless, the pace of sectoral diversification towards a greater share of manufactured exports has been higher in the export flows to

**Table 5. Structure of EC Imports and Exports to/from LA-20 by UCIT Classification, 1981-89**

(percentages)

| UCIT Classif. | 1981 M | X | 1985 M | X | 1986 M | X | 1987 M | X | 1988 M | X | 1989 M | X |
|---|---|---|---|---|---|---|---|---|---|---|---|---|
| UCIT 0 | 36.3 | 5.3 | 35.0 | 4.2 | 43.5 | 5.1 | 37.6 | 4.7 | 36.3 | 5.0 | 33.3 | 6.8 |
| UCIT 1 | 1.2 | 1.9 | 1.7 | 1.2 | 2.2 | 1.5 | 2.0 | 1.5 | 1.7 | 1.8 | 1.6 | 1.7 |
| UCIT 2 | 16.2 | 0.7 | 18.2 | 1.1 | 17.3 | 1.4 | 17.1 | 1.4 | 18.8 | 1.3 | 18.2 | 1.3 |
| UCIT 3 | 26.0 | 0.7 | 23.5 | 1.5 | 13.3 | 0.8 | 15.6 | 1.0 | 9.6 | 0.9 | 10.4 | 1.2 |
| UCIT 4 | 1.1 | 0.1 | 1.7 | 0.1 | 0.9 | 0.4 | 0.6 | 0.3 | 0.5 | 0.5 | 0.8 | 0.6 |
| UCIT 5 | 1.5 | 11.7 | 2.5 | 18.1 | 2.6 | 16.7 | 2.8 | 16.0 | 2.8 | 16.5 | 3.4 | 15.9 |
| UCIT 6 | 10.8 | 16.7 | 11.0 | 11.4 | 13.3 | 12.4 | 13.1 | 12.0 | 16.6 | 11.8 | 19.1 | 11.9 |
| UCIT 7 | 3.9 | 49.0 | 4.4 | 47.0 | 4.1 | 46.8 | 5.9 | 48.0 | 6.4 | 49.7 | 7.3 | 47.0 |
| UCIT 8 | 1.6 | 6.7 | 1.0 | 6.9 | 1.5 | 8.0 | 2.1 | 7.0 | 2.5 | 6.8 | 2.7 | 6.7 |
| UCIT 9 | 1.5 | 7.2 | 1.0 | 8.5 | 1.3 | 6.9 | 3.2 | 8.1 | 4.9 | 5.7 | 3.5 | 6.9 |
| TOTAL | 100.0 | 100.0 | 100.0 | 100.0 | 100.0 | 100.0 | 100.0 | 100.0 | 100.0 | 100.0 | 100.0 | 100.0 |

Note: Figures since 1986 are for EC-12.

UCIT 0: Foodstuffs
UCIT 1: Beverages and tobacco
UCIT 2: Raw materials
UCIT 3: Fuels
UCIT 4: Oils and fats
UCIT 5: Chemicals
UCIT 6: Manufactured goods
UCIT 7: Transport equipment and machinery
UCIT 8: Miscellaneous manufactured articles
UCIT 9: Other

M = Imports
X = Exports

Source: Commission of the European Communities.

trade partners other than the EC. Whereas this share was roughly equal for the United States and the EC in 1970 (11 percent of total exports from the countries of the *Asociación Latinoamericana de Integración*), in 1987 the share was nearly 40 percent for the United States, and less than 21 percent for the EC. In fact, US imports of industrial products from Latin America, measured in US dollars, have grown by nearly 19 percent annually since 1980, as compared with growth rates of about 7 percent and 4.5 percent in the cases of Japan and the EC, respectively. This development is also reflected by the decreasing relevance of the EC within the OECD as an outlet market for Latin American manufactured exports (Table 6).

The increasing relevance of the US market for Latin American manufactured exports is particularly evident in the case of some Mexican products, especially electrical equipment and assembly parts for passenger motor vehicles. Between 1984 and 1989 the annual increase in manufactured products belonging to the forty most relevant commodities exported to the US market was almost 23 percent. This is much higher than the corresponding figure for the forty top commodities as a whole (less than 6 percent) and for total Mexican exports to the United States (6.5 percent). This evolution is attributable to a large extent to the *maquila* sector, which is estimated to account for about 40 percent of Mexican exports to the United States. In spite of the attempts to diversify their production activities and create linkages with the other sectors of the national economy, the dependency of the *maquilas* on fluctuations in the US economy and the world prices of manufactured goods actually reduces the potential benefit that Mexico can draw from this sector.

In a situation similar to that of the US market, Latin American countries have, moreover, suffered a loss in their share of the total manufactured imports of the EC, including traditional products as textiles, to the benefit of other exporting areas, particularly Southeast Asia (Table 7).

One can conclude, therefore, that the SEM effects on commercial relations with Latin America are of less importance than with those regions of Southeast Asia or traditional developed countries where manufactured goods dominate trade relations. In this sense, the effects on Latin America—both positive and negative—will be somewhat marginal, since the SEM will have less effect on primary products than on manufactured products.

A IRELA study on the SEM's impact on Latin American exports to the EC concludes that, on the optimistic assumption of 7 percent growth

**Table 6.   OECD Imports of Industrial Products (SITC 5-8, excluding 68) from the World and from Latin America, 1970, 1980, and 1987**

| SITC Code | Product Groups/ Countries | World | | | LA[a] | | |
|---|---|---|---|---|---|---|---|
| | | 1970 | 1980 | 1987 | 1970 | 1980 | 1987 |
| | | (millions of dollars) | | | | | |
| 5 | Chemicals | 15,170 | 93,572 | 152,560 | 451 | 1,337 | 2,230 |
| 6 | Manufactured goods[b] | 36,675 | 178,404 | 252,184 | 384 | 3,441 | 7,561 |
| 7 | Machinery and transport equipment | 57,148 | 307,626 | 614,327 | 244 | 3,944 | 13,802 |
| 8 | Misc. manufactured articles | 19,266 | 126,015 | 242,174 | 175 | 2,375 | 5,734 |
| | of which: | | | | | | |
| | EC | 69,335 | 411,398 | 651,429 | 304 | 3,244 | 4,595 |
| | USA | 24,152 | 123,362 | 309,102 | 559 | 6,227 | 20,363 |
| | Japan | 5,113 | 27,488 | 56,400 | 54 | 669 | 1,001 |
| | Other | 29,659 | 143,369 | 244,314 | 337 | 957 | 3,368 |
| | | (percentage shares; total = 100) | | | | | |
| | EC | 54.1 | 58.3 | 51.6 | 24.2 | 29.2 | 15.7 |
| | USA | 18.8 | 17.5 | 24.5 | 44.6 | 56.1 | 69.4 |
| | Japan | 4.0 | 3.9 | 4.5 | 4.3 | 6.0 | 3.4 |
| | Other | 23.1 | 20.3 | 19.4 | 26.9 | 8.6 | 11.5 |

[a]Excluding Cuba.
[b]Classified chiefly by material; excluding division 68, i.e. nonferrous metals.

Source: OECD, *Foreign Trade by Commodities*, Vol. II, 1982 and 1987.

in the EC, Latin American exports would be affected—taking trade diversion into account—positively by about 50 percent of their total volume, marginally by 22 percent and negatively by about 28 percent.

Those products (typically industrial) with a higher demand elasticity will benefit relatively more from these growth effects, provided they do not suffer strong trade diversion effects. The eventual downward harmonization of external tariffs and consumption taxes among EC member states could also favor Latin American exports of some food and primary products, particularly if these measures are accompanied by an orientation of consumer preferences towards Latin American products, as seems to be happening with coffee and bananas.

## Table 7. Latin America's Percentage Shares in the Imports of the EC, US, and Japan, 1970, 1980, and 1987

| ISIC Code | Product Groups | EC 1970 | EC 1980 | EC 1987 | USA 1970 | USA 1980 | USA 1987 | Japan 1970 | Japan 1980 | Japan 1987 |
|---|---|---|---|---|---|---|---|---|---|---|
| 321 | Textiles | 2.9 | 7.1 | 5.4 | 4.6 | 9.9 | 8.5 | 2.2 | 2.3 | 2.0 |
| 322 | Wearing apparel | 0.2 | 1.8 | 1.0 | 3.1 | 8.6 | 7.7 | 0.2 | 0.1 | 0.1 |
| 323 | Leather | 16.6 | 16.3 | 9.2 | 13.5 | 17.5 | 14.4 | 5.9 | 2.5 | 1.4 |
| 324 | Footwear | 1.4 | 8.8 | 8.3 | 3.5 | 15.6 | 20.6 | 0.0 | 2.3 | 0.5 |
| 331 | Wood and wood products | 3.0 | 2.9 | 2.7 | 5.0 | 5.7 | 6.7 | 0.2 | 1.3 | 1.2 |
| 332 | Furniture and fixtures | 1.1 | 0.3 | 0.5 | 10.6 | 6.3 | 12.4 | 0.3 | 0.3 | 0.1 |
| 341 | Paper | 0.1 | 2.2 | 2.7 | 0.3 | 2.4 | 5.7 | 0.0 | 7.1 | 4.8 |
| 342 | Printing and publishing | 1.3 | 1.6 | 1.4 | 3.9 | 4.6 | 2.5 | 0.3 | 0.1 | 0.2 |
| 351 | Industrial chemicals | 2.1 | 2.0 | 2.1 | 2.7 | 4.6 | 5.9 | 2.0 | 2.8 | 2.0 |
| 352 | Other chemical products | 3.2 | 2.0 | 1.9 | 7.3 | 5.2 | 4.5 | 1.2 | 0.7 | 0.5 |
| 355 | Rubber products | 0.5 | 1.4 | 1.9 | 2.5 | 0.8 | 4.9 | 0.0 | 0.4 | 0.3 |
| 356 | Plastic products | 0.1 | 0.4 | 0.5 | 4.0 | 2.8 | 2.9 | 0.0 | 0.3 | 0.1 |
| 361 | Pottery, china, earthware | 0.1 | 1.3 | 2.3 | 1.6 | 4.3 | 6.6 | 0.9 | 0.5 | 0.6 |
| 362 | Glass and glass products | 0.4 | 0.7 | 1.2 | 2.7 | 5.1 | 11.2 | 0.1 | 1.2 | 0.2 |
| 369 | Other non-met. products | 0.1 | 0.9 | 1.4 | 6.8 | 9.2 | 14.1 | 0.7 | 1.1 | 0.5 |
| 371 | Iron and steel | 1.0 | 4.5 | 5.5 | 2.0 | 4.8 | 9.5 | 4.8 | 9.5 | 14.2 |
| 381 | Metal products | 0.3 | 0.6 | 0.6 | 1.7 | 3.7 | 4.9 | 0.0 | 0.3 | 0.2 |
| 382R | Machinery | 0.2 | 0.6 | 0.7 | 0.8 | 2.2 | 4.4 | 0.0 | 0.6 | 0.2 |
| 3825 | Office, EDP | 1.5 | 1.0 | 0.3 | 5.8 | 5.2 | 2.9 | 0.1 | 10.8 | 3.5 |
| 383 | Electrical machinery | 0.2 | 0.5 | 0.7 | 4.4 | 12.0 | 11.5 | 0.0 | 0.3 | 0.3 |
| 3843 | Motor vehicles | 0.7 | 3.2 | 3.6 | 0.3 | 1.5 | 4.4 | 0.0 | 2.8 | 0.2 |
| 384R | Other transp. equip. | 0.5 | 1.5 | 2.3 | 1.8 | 1.9 | 5.1 | 0.0 | 1.6 | 0.3 |
| 385 | Precision engineer. | 0.1 | 0.2 | 0.2 | 0.6 | 3.2 | 3.6 | 0.0 | 0.1 | 0.1 |
| 390 | Other manufacturing | 1.9 | 1.0 | 1.3 | 2.7 | 5.2 | 5.0 | 4.8 | 3.9 | 2.7 |
| | Subtotal SITC 6-8 (excl. 68) | 1.2 | 2.2 | 1.9 | 2.3 | 5.0 | 6.6 | 1.0 | 2.4 | 1.8 |
| 311/2 | Food products | 28.6 | 29.1 | 28.2 | 39.5 | 44.6 | 34.2 | 11.3 | 10.5 | 8.4 |
| 313 | Beverages | 1.0 | 2.6 | 4.2 | 0.7 | 2.9 | 7.6 | 0.6 | 0.7 | 1.8 |
| 314 | Tobacco manufactures | 0.3 | 1.4 | 0.8 | 7.0 | 37.5 | 32.4 | 0.0 | 0.0 | 0.0 |
| 353/4 | Petroleum refineries | 5.5 | 7.4 | 1.3 | 42.8 | 31.1 | 30.6 | 2.3 | 1.9 | 0.7 |
| 372 | Nonferrous metals | 14.5 | 12.9 | 11.8 | 17.4 | 15.2 | 16.6 | 11.3 | 17.7 | 15.3 |
| | Subtotal other manuf. prod. | 21.2 | 17.8 | 16.3 | 31.5 | 30.5 | 26.7 | 8.8 | 8.9 | 7.2 |
| | Total | 8.0 | 6.0 | 5.6 | 12.0 | 12.3 | 10.9 | 6.5 | 3.8 | 4.0 |

Source: OECD, *Foreign Trade by Commodities*.

The greater attention given to environmental problems by the EC may also lead to the establishment of stricter rules on environmental control for refineries and mineral processing industries, thus stimulating indirectly the relocation of these plants towards raw materials exporting countries, including Latin America.

SEM-related measures are also likely to be aimed at gradually phasing out subsidies of large energy consumers in metal processing, thus similarly contributing to the improvement of the competitive position of Latin American smelters. Typically, only one or two countries account for each mineral product exported to the EC from Latin America. For instance, in 1988, Brazil supplied 100 percent of the region's iron ore and refined tin exports to the EC, and 86 percent of primary aluminium exports; Chile provided, in turn, 82 percent of copper exports.

In some cases, imports of commodities and services from Latin America will have to face new difficulties due to the establishment of common technical and health norms and regulations. In the service sector, the creation of the SEM in areas such as transport, insurance, finance, and marketing will probably imvoke the application of rules of reciprocity with third countries, a condition that is less feasible in the case of Latin American countries because of differences in quality standards and costs. Measures geared to protect the environment (e.g., air traffic noise regulation) are also likely to restrict or impede the capacity of Latin American service industries to expand their activities into the EC market.

Latin American countries will be able to draw some benefit from the SEM as long as their exports achieve a higher price and quality competitiveness. This scenario appears more realistic for middle-income countries with a larger and more diversified productive structure, and which are in a stronger position to establish trade and investment links with other regions of the world. These countries, however, may have to overcome problems of regional adjustment for similar products in the European countries. In view of the stronger competition likely to come from the rapidly growing economies of Southeast Asia and the increased need to adapt to the enlarged market created by the SEM, these countries should endeavour to further diversify their exports and provide them with better marketing facilities.

## US-Latin American Trade: Recent Trends and the Impact of the SEM

Compared to EC-Latin American trade relations, Latin American countries (LA-20) have a higher share of US trade flows. In addition, the US market constitutes a relatively more important trading partner for those countries. In 1988, LA-20 represented nearly 11 percent of total US imports and 12 percent of total US exports (Tables 8 and 9). Although clearly declining in comparison to the beginning of the 1970s, the LA-20 share still represents nearly one-third of developing countries' trade with the United States. If intra-regional trade is included, the United States, in turn, covers an increasing percentage of Latin American trade over the 1980s. This percentage exceeded 40 percent in the second half of the decade (Table 10).

In terms of performance in the 1980s, relative to other trading partner areas of the United States, Latin American exports have shown a more dynamic growth than exports of the Middle East and Africa, but a slower pace of growth than Asian and industrial countries' exports to the United States. On the whole, in spite of the increasing concentration of

Table 8. Participation of LA-20 in Total Imports and in Imports from Developing Countries of EC-12 and US, 1970-88

(values in percentage of total)

| Year | EC-12 | | US | |
| | Extra EC-12 | Developing Countries | World | Developing Countries |
|------|------|------|------|------|
| 1970 | 8.10 | 21.29 | 11.96 | 45.75 |
| 1975 | 5.94 | 13.00 | 11.92 | 28.39 |
| 1980 | 5.90 | 12.90 | 12.19 | 25.55 |
| 1981 | 6.47 | 14.25 | 12.27 | 27.73 |
| 1982 | 6.59 | 15.26 | 13.31 | 30.63 |
| 1983 | 7.30 | 18.00 | 13.82 | 32.46 |
| 1984 | 7.24 | 18.63 | 12.98 | 32.51 |
| 1985 | 7.45 | 19.42 | 12.58 | 34.15 |
| 1986 | 6.08 | 18.88 | 10.74 | 30.49 |
| 1987 | 5.78 | 18.11 | 10.95 | 28.58 |
| 1988 | 6.04 | 20.11 | 11.13 | 28.81 |
| 1989 | 5.90 | 19.60 | n.a. | n.a. |

Sources: EC-12 = Calculated on the basis of figures from EUROSTAT, *External Trade Statistical Yearbook*, Bruxelles-Luxembourg: EUROSTAT (1988); EUROSTAT, *External Trade Monthly Statistics*, Bruxelles-Luxembourg: EUROSTAT (1989). US = Calculated on the basis of figures from IMF, *Direction of Trade Statistics*, Washington, DC: IMF (1976, 1987, 1989).

Table 9. Participation of LA 20 in Total Exports and in Exports to Developing Countries of EC-12 and US, 1970-88

(values in percentage of total trade)

| Year | EC-12 Extra EC-12 | EC-12 Developing Countries | World | US Developing Countries |
|------|------|------|------|------|
| 1970 | 7.21 | 23.26 | 13.18 | 43.91 |
| 1975 | 7.08 | 18.38 | 14.49 | 38.00 |
| 1980 | 6.35 | 15.41 | 16.33 | 41.14 |
| 1981 | 6.38 | 14.29 | 16.66 | 40.72 |
| 1982 | 5.37 | 12.25 | 14.18 | 32.87 |
| 1983 | 4.27 | 10.38 | 11.28 | 28.15 |
| 1984 | 4.29 | 11.47 | 12.07 | 31.48 |
| 1985 | 4.11 | 12.07 | 13.07 | 34.62 |
| 1986 | 4.24 | 13.49 | 12.87 | 35.73 |
| 1987 | 4.10 | 13.30 | 12.49 | 35.03 |
| 1988 | 3.79 | 12.12 | 12.51 | 33.93 |

Source: EC-12 = Calculated on the basis of figures from EUROSTAT, *External Trade Statistical Yearbook*, Bruxelles-Luxembourg: EUROSTAT (1988); EUROSTAT, *External Trade Monthly Statistics*, Bruxelles-Luxembourg: EUROSTAT (1989). US = Calculated on the basis of figures from IMF, *Direction of Trade Statistics*, Washington, DC: IMF (1976, 1987, 1989).

Latin American exports to the US market over the last decade, the countries of the region have not drawn any remarkable benefit from the import expansion of the United States in the early 1980s. Latin American countries thus lost the first position that they held among developing regions as a major supplier to the United States, while Southeast Asian countries increased their share substantially.[13]

Unlike EC-Latin American trade, the participation of Latin America in total US trade flows is higher in exports than in imports. The same result is also maintained relative to US trade with developing countries. In other words, while Latin American countries contribute relatively more to US exports than to US imports, EC-Latin American trade relations are characterized by the opposite performance. Nevertheless, whereas in the former case US imports from Latin America grew by about 4 percent a year in the period 1980-88, the corresponding figure

## Table 10. Participation of EC-12, US, and LA-20 in the Trade of LA-20, 1970-88

(values in percentage of total trade)

| Year | Imports from | | | Exports to | | |
|------|-------|------|-------|-------|------|-------|
|      | EC-12 | US   | LA-20 | EC-12 | US   | LA-20 |
| 1970 | 27.3  | 39.7 | 13.1  | 31.3  | 30.9 | 11.9  |
| 1975 | 24.2  | 33.9 | 13.3  | 25.5  | 28.5 | 16.6  |
| 1980 | 19.1  | 34.1 | 14.7  | 23.8  | 30.0 | 16.3  |
| 1981 | 18.0  | 35.1 | 15.4  | 22.4  | 28.4 | 16.4  |
| 1982 | 17.6  | 33.0 | 17.9  | 23.4  | 31.3 | 15.0  |
| 1983 | 16.7  | 31.0 | 19.2  | 23.3  | 34.9 | 11.8  |
| 1984 | 16.4  | 32.2 | 20.3  | 21.8  | 38.5 | 12.1  |
| 1985 | 17.5  | 35.5 | 18.2  | 22.9  | 38.7 | 11.6  |
| 1986 | 20.9  | 35.5 | 16.6  | 22.8  | 38.5 | 12.8  |
| 1987 | 19.4  | 39.5 | 14.5  | 20.0  | 43.5 | 11.8  |
| 1988 | 17.7  | 42.8 | 13.9  | 21.1  | 41.2 | 11.0  |

Source: Calculated on the basis of figures from IMF, *Direction of Trade Statistics*, Washington, DC: IMF (1976, 1987, 1989).

for EC imports is less than 1 percent (according to International Monetary Fund trade statistics).

With regard to individual countries' trade, the orientation of trade flows towards the US market is particularly notable in some Latin American countries: Mexico, Honduras, the Dominican Republic, and Haiti show a high and increasing dependence on US imports at a level equivalent to more than half of the imports of those countries in 1988 (Table 11). Similarly, Mexico, the Dominican Republic, and Haiti send more than half of their exports to the US market (Table 12). In absolute terms, both US import and export flows are highly concentrated with three main trading partners—Mexico, Brazil, and Venezuela—which together account for approximately 75 percent of total US-Latin American trade. Mexico's share, by far the largest, increased over the last decade.

The above considerations underline the high dependence and increasing concentration of Latin American countries towards the United States as a major trade partner in recent years, in contrast with the

Table 11. Participation of EC-12, US, and LA-20 in the Imports of LA-20, 1980-88

| Country | EC-12 1980 | 1985 | 1988 | US 1980 | 1985 | 1988 | LA-20 1980 | 1985 | 1988 |
|---|---|---|---|---|---|---|---|---|---|
| Mexico | 14.9 | 13.0 | 9.7 | 61.6 | 66.6 | 74.9 | 4.1 | 4.6 | 1.6 |
| Guatemala | 13.9 | 13.8 | 17.7 | 34.5 | 31.2 | 43.0 | 29.1 | 39.9 | 22.2 |
| Honduras | 11.7 | 14.6 | 10.5 | 42.4 | 41.0 | 56.8 | 26.5 | 30.2 | 13.0 |
| El Salvador | 9.5 | 10.5 | 10.0 | 20.0 | 33.9 | 42.3 | 62.5 | 44.7 | 31.3 |
| Nicaragua | 8.9 | 24.8 | 29.4 | 27.5 | 8.5 | 1.3 | 55.6 | 32.8 | 29.2 |
| Costa Rica | 13.4 | 15.1 | 12.9 | 34.3 | 34.7 | 39.0 | 31.4 | 31.1 | 30.9 |
| Panama | 7.1 | 8.3 | 10.6 | 33.8 | 31.5 | 18.7 | 17.8 | 28.6 | 9.8 |
| Cuba | 39.2 | 26.2 | 31.2 | 0.0 | 0.0 | 0.2 | 10.4 | 28.9 | 13.6 |
| Haiti | 11.4 | 11.8 | 12.3 | 53.4 | 62.2 | 62.0 | 4.3 | 5.7 | 3.6 |
| Dominican Rep. | 10.5 | 10.0 | 9.4 | 44.8 | 33.7 | 56.3 | 25.6 | 40.7 | 21.0 |
| Colombia | 20.4 | 19.6 | 20.5 | 39.5 | 35.3 | 36.7 | 16.1 | 23.5 | 16.3 |
| Venezuela | 23.6 | 23.1 | 26.6 | 47.8 | 47.5 | 44.0 | 8.9 | 10.8 | 11.2 |
| Ecuador | 17.9 | 21.9 | 20.8 | 35.6 | 30.5 | 33.1 | 12.4 | 19.5 | 18.8 |
| Peru | 17.9 | 23.4 | 21.8 | 29.7 | 28.2 | 29.9 | 11.2 | 25.4 | 29.6 |
| Brazil | 16.5 | 14.6 | 21.6 | 18.6 | 19.7 | 20.9 | 11.8 | 12.3 | 12.5 |
| Chile | 19.9 | 19.6 | 19.5 | 28.6 | 21.3 | 19.7 | 24.5 | 25.5 | 26.8 |
| Bolivia | 19.3 | 18.7 | 12.5 | 28.5 | 20.6 | 21.0 | 27.9 | 46.5 | 56.8 |
| Paraguay | 17.0 | 16.1 | 20.0 | 9.9 | 7.9 | 10.1 | 51.3 | 55.4 | 43.5 |
| Uruguay | 19.1 | 16.7 | 20.9 | 9.8 | 7.6 | 7.9 | 37.0 | 35.5 | 50.7 |
| Argentina | 29.7 | 28.0 | 27.5 | 22.6 | 18.2 | 18.8 | 21.2 | 34.6 | 32.7 |

Source: Calculated on the basis of figures from IMF, *Direction of Trade Statistics,* Washington, DC: IMF (1987, 1989).

apparent diversification of the 1970s. From 1980 to 1987 the US trade deficit increased from $25 billion to almost $160 billion as a consequence of a severe slowdown of export growth and a continuous upward trend of imports (between 1982 and 1986, US imports increased in volume by 60 percent, while US exports grew by only 6 percent). Among other reasons, the lower levels of external demand in the highly indebted Latin American countries contributed to this performance. Some estimates attribute 10-20 percent of the US trade deficit to the serious economic problems of Latin America.[14] This negative trend, however, appears to have reversed during the late 1980s. Between 1987 and the first half of 1990, US export volume increased 72 percent, while US import volume

## Table 12. Participation of EC-12, US, and LA-20 in the Exports of LA-20, 1980-88

| Country | EC-12 | | | US | | | LA-20 | | |
|---|---|---|---|---|---|---|---|---|---|
| | 1980 | 1985 | 1988 | 1980 | 1985 | 1988 | 1980 | 1985 | 1988 |
| Mexico | 15.3 | 18.2 | 9.1 | 65.4 | 60.4 | 72.9 | 6.0 | 5.4 | 4.3 |
| Guatemala | 25.0 | 15.3 | 19.2 | 7.7 | 36.2 | 40.2 | 32.5 | 24.7 | 19.0 |
| Honduras | 24.5 | 25.8 | 23.9 | 52.8 | 49.9 | 49.4 | 12.6 | 5.2 | 5.7 |
| El Salvador | 20.2 | 25.7 | 27.1 | 41.0 | 48.2 | 39.4 | 28.6 | 17.1 | 19.2 |
| Nicaragua | 34.6 | 32.7 | 32.1 | 38.7 | 15.0 | 0.4 | 19.7 | 7.8 | 13.1 |
| Costa Rica | 23.7 | 23.5 | 25.8 | 33.8 | 39.5 | 44.4 | 34.1 | 22.4 | 16.4 |
| Panama | 12.9 | 16.2 | 21.1 | 49.3 | 64.1 | 49.5 | 18.3 | 12.0 | 16.6 |
| Cuba | 30.4 | 32.0 | 28.7 | 0.0 | 0.0 | 0.0 | 8.9 | 6.3 | 5.2 |
| Haiti | 38.3 | 13.2 | 10.7 | 56.6 | 82.1 | 84.8 | 0.7 | 1.5 | 1.0 |
| Dominican Rep. | 10.2 | 13.2 | 8.9 | 52.2 | 76.2 | 79.3 | 10.1 | 1.5 | 1.1 |
| Colombia | 36.8 | 34.8 | 28.6 | 27.1 | 32.8 | 40.4 | 16.4 | 11.9 | 11.9 |
| Venezuela | 17.4 | 20.2 | 11.1 | 27.7 | 46.0 | 48.9 | 12.4 | 13.9 | 13.3 |
| Ecuador | 8.0 | 4.4 | 9.2 | 32.6 | 57.1 | 45.9 | 19.3 | 9.3 | 14.7 |
| Peru | 20.0 | 22.5 | 29.6 | 32.1 | 33.9 | 21.7 | 17.9 | 13.9 | 15.0 |
| Brazil | 30.5 | 26.9 | 27.7 | 17.4 | 27.1 | 25.8 | 17.8 | 9.5 | 11.6 |
| Chile | 37.1 | 33.5 | 36.1 | 12.6 | 22.5 | 19.7 | 24.3 | 14.3 | 12.7 |
| Bolivia | 24.4 | 20.9 | 18.4 | 25.7 | 14.1 | 17.2 | 36.7 | 60.2 | 54.8 |
| Paraguay | 30.8 | 50.1 | 30.6 | 5.5 | 1.3 | 3.6 | 45.4 | 32.1 | 29.3 |
| Uruguay | 31.4 | 22.6 | 26.2 | 7.8 | 15.1 | 11.3 | 37.3 | 27.8 | 27.3 |
| Argentina | 30.4 | 24.5 | 30.5 | 8.9 | 12.2 | 15.3 | 24.3 | 21.9 | 17.9 |

Source: Calculated on the basis of figures from IMF, *Direction of Trade Statistics*, Washington DC: IMF (1987, 1989).

increased by only 21 percent, leading to a progressive shrinking of the trade deficit to an annualized $92 billion in the first half of 1990.

In Latin America, the opposite tendency in external trade can be identified over the last decade, with export growth being higher than import growth, coupled with a slowdown of GDP growth in most countries. Consequently, the US trade balance with Latin America changed from a surplus of $1.3 billion in 1980 to a deficit of some $18.6 billion in 1984, which decreased to $7.8 billion in 1988 in line with the overall trend.[15] The US adjustment process, aimed at achieving better internal and external equilibrium, is likely to require a further import contraction in the early 1990s, with particularly negative implications for those Latin American countries that currently enjoy a trade surplus with the United States, such as Brazil, Mexico, and Venezuela.

The persistent, though declining, US trade deficit suggests, at least for the beginning of the 1990s, that there will be no sustained Latin American export growth in the US market, especially in view of the higher oil prices in international markets. The sectoral composition of trade flows nonetheless seems to have proceeded towards a greater balance. On the one hand, manufactured, especially non-traditional products, have attained the highest growth of Latin American exports to the US market. On the other hand, US agricultural and raw material-based exports to Latin America have grown faster than the exports of manufactured products.[16] Nevertheless, while US exports to the world and to the EC have been sectorally concentrated approximately to the same extent as imports, with regard to Latin American trade flows, US exports still appear relatively more concentrated in a few main commodities on the import side, despite the significant decline of imports of crude oil and oil products. A similar picture arises if one examines US trade relations with with Mexico, its main Latin American trade partner (Table 13).

President George Bush's administration is particularly interested in giving priority to trade relations with Latin America. This openness is clearly evident in the similar proposals from the United States and Latin America for the elimination of agricultural subsidies in the framework of the current GATT negotiations. More broadly, the recent proposals put forward within the Enterprise for the Americas Initiative (EAI) include the restructuring of the Latin American official debt to the US government, the supply of additional funds to the Inter-American Development Bank for the promotion of direct investment in the region, and in the long term, the setting up of a free trade area, provided that Latin American countries adhere to their structural adjustment and trade liberalization programs. Import barriers are likely to persist for steel products, temperate food items, patents for medical equipment, and sugar, thus hindering the exports of several Latin American countries.[17]

Along with similar initiatives recently undertaken at the subregional level, the EAI can be considered as a further attempt to improve the efficiency and potential growth of the productive structures of the partner countries involved by better exploring economies of scale and comparative advantages.[18] Estimates on the static effects of the elimination of trade barriers attribute an eventual 7.2 percent increase of export

## Table 13. Sectoral Concentration of US Trade Flows, 1984 and 1988

| | 1984 | 1988 | | 1984 | 1988 |
|---|---|---|---|---|---|
| $X^W$ | 68.4 | 69.8 | $M^W$ | 64.5 | 66.0 |
| $X^W_{(3)}$ | 12.9 | 14.3 | $M^W_{(3)}$ | 25.6 | 19.9 |
| $X^{EC}$ | 72.2 | 75.8 | $M^{EC}$ | 67.5 | 67.7 |
| $X^{EC}_{(3)}$ | 18.9 | 22.9 | $M^{EC}_{(3)}$ | 20.2 | 15.9 |
| $X^{LA}$ | 67.1 | 67.5 | $M^{LA}$ | 82.0 | 74.9 |
| $X^{LA}_{(3)}$ | 12.5 | 12.6 | $M^{LA}_{(3)}$ | 46.5 | 25.1 |
| $X^{Mex}$ | 72.2 | 72.6 | $M^{Mex}$ | 84.7 | 81.2 |
| $X^{Mex(3)}$ | 17.8 | 16.3 | $X^{Mex(3)}$ | 45.5 | 23.2 |

Notes:
$X^W$: percentage in total US exports to the world (top 40 commodities).
$X^W_{(3)}$: percentage in total US exports to the world (top 3 commodities).
$X^{EC}$: percentage in total US exports to EC (top 40 commodities).
$X^{EC}_{(3)}$: percentage in total US exports to EC (top 3 commodities).
$X^{LA}$: percentage in total US exports to LA (top 40 commodities).
$X^{LA}_{(3)}$: percentage in total US exports to LA (top 3 commodities).
$X^{Mex}$: percentage in total US exports to Mexico (top 40 commodities).
$X^{Mex(3)}$: percentage in total US exports to Mexico (top 3 commodities).
$M^W$: percentage in total US imports from the world (top 40 commodities).
$M^W_{(3)}$: percentage in total US imports from the world (top 3 commodities).
$M^{EC}$: percentage in total US imports from EC (top 40 commodities).
$M^{EC}_{(3)}$: percentage in total US imports from EC (top 3 commodities).
$M^{LA}$: percentage in total US imports from LA (top 40 commodities).
$M^{LA}_{(3)}$: percentage in total US imports from LA (top 3 commodities).
$M^{Mex}$: percentage in total US imports from Mexico (top 40 commodities).
$M^{Mex(3)}$: percentage in total US imports from Mexico (top 3 commodities).
LA: Western Hemisphere (excluding Cuba).

Source: Calculated on the basis of figures from US Department of Commerce: *US Foreign Trade Highlights 1988*, International Trade Administration (July 1989).

earnings for Latin American countries relative to their total exports. Moreover, these estimates do not include improved conditions resulting from possible trade diversion due to the substitutability in the US market of some items produced in and exported from other regions relative to similar Latin American products. The former would in fact suffer from a comparative disadvantage brought about by the free trade-induced changes in relative prices.[19]

Within the above framework, the SEM certainly will have an impact on US-Latin American trade. The additional income effect brought about by the SEM in EC countries will positively affect aggregate import demand, including demand of imports from the United States and Latin America. If both trade partners are able to respond effectively to this increased demand, they will profit from increased export growth and hence eventually stimulate their own inter-regional trade.

At the same time, a more productive and efficient industrial structure in the EC might compete more successfully with US firms, not only within the EC, but also in the United States and in third country markets. In view of the low levels of growth expected for other developing regions, this may particularly concern some Latin American and Asian countries. The resulting competition will be felt more the higher the elasticity of substitution between US and European products.

In recent years, many US companies have reduced their investment activities or even divested in several Latin American countries, while European firms have, on the whole, tended to strengthen their presence in the region, as highlighted in section one with reference to foreign investment flows. Nevertheless, the recent attention of European investors to Eastern European countries may reduce the potential for renewed investment flows to Latin America in the long run.

For specific products, the emphasis of the SEM on deregulation and competition, which also implies the dismantling of bilateral preferential trade agreements of individual member states with extra-EC suppliers, is likely to effect a gradual shift of EC imports towards geographically closer exporters, provided that similar price and quality conditions are met. A case in point might be the eventual increased orientation of EC import demand towards the Mediterranean countries for products that have so far constituted a substantial share of Latin American exports to the EC, such as agricultural and food items.

Thus, a greater concentration of Latin American exports on their "traditional" outlet market is bound to follow. In this regard, it is relevant to try to assess the potential of growth of Latin American exports to the US market. Alternative regression equations have been applied on the period 1970-88, and have subsequently been used for forecasting Latin American total exports to the United States on the basis of projections of total US imports for the first half of the 1990s. According to the different results of these analyses, in the period 1988-95 Latin American exports to the United States would increase by a rate ranging between 0.3 and 6.9 percent per year, which would, therefore, represent either a substantial deterioration, which seems unlikely to happen to this extent, or alternatively an improvement if compared with about 4.1 percent of yearly growth in the period 1980-88. The corresponding growth rates for total US imports are about 7.5 and 5 percent for the last decade and the following forecasting period, respectively.

According to the most pessimistic results of the regression analyses, corresponding to those of equation (2) in the appendix, Latin American exports to the United States would undergo a slowdown in their growth pace until reaching negative growth rates in the last three years of the forecast period. On the other hand, under the most favorable outlook envisaged by the forecasting exercises, Latin America would represent nearly 13 percent of US imports in 1995, a level nearly equivalent to the average figure achieved in the 1980s.

## Perspectives for the Future

In spite of the declining participation of the EC market in total Latin American exports over the last two decades, this market will continue to significantly affect the evolution of Latin American exports, especially in the case of those countries like Chile for which the EC represents an important share of its export market. The analysis in the preceding sections has stressed the existence of some specific problems in these trade relations, such as the structural asymmetry in terms of sectoral composition of flows and their concentration in few major products and countries.

The SEM's implementation is expected to bring about positive and negative implications for Latin American trade relations, the result depending on various aspects, which include regulatory changes, income and price effects, evolution of the internal demand, and transformations in the production structure. The overall assessment should not overlook substantial differences among individual products and specific countries as well as their capacity to obtain a greater bargaining power through their subregional integration processes.

Furthermore, other factors along with the SEM can be expected to contribute to a reshaping of the Latin American position in the world economy. The still pending outcome of GATT negotiations, the political and economic changes occurring in Eastern Europe, the Persian Gulf Crisis, and finally, the capability of Latin American countries themselves to effectively carry out, without excessive social costs, their structural adjustment programs.

On the whole, even though for the first time in GATT negotiations, discussions have been held dealing with topics of particular concern to developing countries, no substantial resolutions have so far been taken in these themes, and, therefore, there is a risk of a further strengthening of large trading blocs in different world regions, such as the case eventually promoted by the EAI. In Europe, this process is already apparent in East-West economic relations, especially with the inclusion of Hungary and Poland in the EC GSP and the elimination of almost all EC import quotas restricting trade of industrial goods from those countries as well as from Bulgaria and Czechoslovakia. A following phase could envisage the establishment of association agreements with this group of countries.

For Latin America, the changes in Eastern Europe could have a diversionary impact, especially in direct investment flows from the EC, whereas trade flows might be affected only in the long run. In the latter case, however, it is possible to foresee positive effects for the demand of certain Latin American products, particularly tropical foodstuffs.

In order to partly offset the negative impact of trade and investment diversion due to the SEM, the EC will not pay compensations to the developing countries eventually suffering from these losses, but it is likely to put more emphasis on technical cooperation.[20] In Latin America, the EC contribution in this respect appears to still lie at modest levels, but it seems to have undergone improvements in quality, by better focusing on priority targets and least developed countries and regions. This contribution seems appropriate in view of the limited scope for increased Latin American participation in their principal external outlet market in the coming few years, as indicated by the projections of Latin American exports to the United States.

# Appendix[21]

In order to obtain projections for total US imports, a logarithmic auto-regressive trend model has been applied on the estimation period, with results given in equation (1) below. A predictive failure test applied on the last two years of the time series is used for the extrapolation points at robust and significant estimates. The Durbin-h test is also significant at the 5 percent level. T-statistics are given in brackets, under the estimated parameters.

The results thus obtained have been applied in three alternative forecasting equations by assuming Latin American (Western Hemisphere) exports to the United States depending on the overall import demand of the country. Equation (2) uses the proportionate rate of change expressed as the difference of annual logarithm values. For equations (3) and (4) the Cochrane-Orcutt procedure has been applied to remove positive autoregressive processes in the estimated residuals (the Durbin-Watson test is inconclusive though). The root mean sum of square of prediction errors of the last two equations concerning the last two years of the real time series (1987 and 1988) seems to point at slightly better results when using equation (3).

*Results of Forecasts (millions of dollars)*

|               | (1)   | (2)   | (3)   | (4)   |
|---------------|-------|-------|-------|-------|
| 1988 (actual) | 459.9 | 53.7  | 53.7  | 53.7  |
| 1992          | 571.3 | 56.06 | 67.73 | 74.78 |
| 1995          | 647.4 | 54.93 | 76.48 | 85.73 |

$$\log(M_{US}) = 0.49 + 0.93 \log(M_{US})_{-1} \qquad R^2 = 0.98 \qquad (1)$$
$$\phantom{\log(M_{US}) = } (2.97) \quad\ (28.91) \qquad\qquad Dh = -0.89$$

$$r(MLA_{US}) = -0.065 + 1.39\ r(M_{US}) \qquad R^2 = 0.70 \qquad (2)$$
$$\phantom{r(MLA_{US}) = } (-1.68) \quad\ (6.11) \qquad\qquad DW = 1.63$$

$$MLA_{US} = 7.36 + 0.11\ M_{US} \qquad R^2 = 0.97 \qquad (3)$$
$$\phantom{MLA_{US} = } (1.10) \quad\ (5.53) \qquad\qquad DW = 1.53$$

$$\log(MLA_{US}) = -1.80 + 0.97 \log(M_{US}) \qquad R^2 = 0.98 \qquad (4)$$
$$\phantom{\log(MLA_{US}) = } (-3.17) \quad\ (9.35) \qquad\qquad DW = 1.43$$

---

$M_{US}$ = US imports
$MLA_{US}$ = US imports from Latin America

# Notes

1. Wolf Grabendorff, "European Community Relations with Latin America: Policy without Illusions," *Journal of Interamerican Studies and World Affairs* 4 (1987-88): 69-87.

2. European Community, *Guidelines for Cooperation with the Developing Countries in Latin America and Asia*, COM(90)176, Brussels, June 1990.

3. *Fostering Foreign Direct Investment in Latin America*, Institute of International Finance (Washington DC, July 1990).

4. See A. R. Blair, "The Relationship of MNC Direct Investment to Host Country Trade and Trade Policy: Some Preliminary Evidence," in *Governments and Multinationals. The Policy of Control versus Autonomy*, ed. W. H. Goldberg (Cambridge, Mass.: Oelgeschlager, Gun & Hair, 1983); Bernard Lietaer, *Europe, Latin America, the Multinationals. A Positive Sum Game for the Exchange of Raw Materials and Technology in the 1980s* (Westmead, Gower, 1979); and UNCTC, *Transnational Corporations and International Trade: An Empirical Analysis* (New York: United Nations, 1984).

5. Georg Koopmann, "Handelspolitik der EG im Zeichen des Binnenmarktes," *Wirtschaftsdienst* 8 (1989).

6. Julius Rosenblatt et al., *The Common Agricultural Policy of the European Community, Principles and Consequences*, International Monetary Fund (Washington, DC, November 1988).

7. CEPAL, "Ronda de Uruguay. Hacia una posición latinoamericana sobre los productos agrícolas," *Comercio Exterior*, 6 (Mexico City, 1989): 458-84.

8. CEPAL, *Europa 1992 y sus consecuencias económicas sobre América Latina* (Santiago, September 1990): 11-17.

9. Deutsches Institut für Wirtschaftsforschung, "EG-Binnenmarkt und Handelspolitik gegenüber Entwicklungsländern," *Wochenbericht* (June 1989): 245-53.

10. IRELA, *Documento de Base - Relaciones entre la Comunidad Europea y América Latina: Balance y perspectivas (Febrero 1989-Marzo 1991)* (Madrid, 1991).

11. CEPAL, *Exportaciones latinoamericanas de productos básicos: situación y perspectivas*, LC/R 778 (Santiago, 1989).

12. CEPAL, *Las políticas macroeconómicas de la Comunidad Europea y sus efectos sobre las economías latinoamericanas y del Caribe* (Santiago, September 1990)

13. Carlos Juan Moneta, "Relaciones comerciales y financieras de América Latina con Japón y Estados Unidos: el papel del comercio, la asistencia y los flujos financieros," *Integración Latinoamericana* 144 (Buenos Aires, April 1989): 11-22.

14. Willy de Clercq, "The United States and the European Community: Brothers yet Foes?" *European Affairs* 3 (Autumn 1987): 16-24.

15. Roberto Bouzas and Juan Carlos Barboza, *Las relaciones económicas entre Estados Unidos y los países de América Latina y el Caribe en 1989*, FLACSO (Buenos Aires, 1990).

16. George C. Georgiu and Francisco E. Thoumi, "Corrientes comerciales entre Estados Unidos y América Latina: 1967-1985," *Integración Latinoamericana* 144 (Buenos Aires, April 1989): 23-30.

17. Sistema Económico Latinoamericano, "The Bush Enterprise for the Americas Initiative: A Preliminary Analysis by the SELA Permanent Secretariat," SELA Doc. (Caracas, September 1990).

18. Ariel Davrieux, "Prospects for the Re-establishment of Economic Growth in Latin America," International Forum on Latin American Perspectives, IDB-OECD (Paris, November 1990): 21-23.

19. CEPAL, *América Latina frente a la Iniciativa Bush: un examen inicial* (Santiago, September 1990).

20. Jürgen Wiemann, *The Implications of the Uruguay Round and the Single Market for the European Community's Trade Policy towards Developing Countries*, German Development Institute (Berlin, 1990).

21. Prepared by Stefano Mainardi. The statistical information has been drawn from *Direction of Trade Statistics*, IMF (Washington, DC, various years).

# Europe Can Help, but Will It?

*Henry R. Nau*

Latin America is identified with development strategies that put little emphasis on trade benefits. While the world trading system was liberalizing in an unprecedented fashion in the 1950s and 1960s, Latin American countries pursued import substitution strategies and trade stagnated. When a few Latin American countries, principally Brazil, became more export-oriented in the 1970s and 1980s, the world trading system came under severe strain as a result of oil and interest rate shocks. Not surprisingly, Latin American trade today represents only about 4 percent of total world trade.

What benefits the Latin American countries have derived from trade, they have derived more from US rather than European or Japanese markets. If one assumes that manufacturing trade yields higher benefits than commodity trade, the United States in 1987 absorbed almost 70 percent of Latin America's industrial exports to the countries of the Organisation for Economic Cooperation and Development, compared to 15.7 percent and 3.4 percent for the European Community (EC) and Japan respectively. Moreover, the US number was up from 44.6 percent in 1970, while the number for both the EC and Japan was down for the same period from earlier levels of 24 and 4 percent respectively (see Table 3 in Wolf Grabendorff's paper).

Are these patterns likely to change? In the early 1990s, many more Latin American countries are turning to liberalized trade and market-oriented economic policies. The world trading system, despite severe strains, has expanded steadily in the 1980s, growing annually at rates of 5 percent or more since 1985. The announcement that the United States will seek free trade agreements with Latin American countries promises further expansion. General political conditions have improved with the end of the Cold War and the trend toward greater openness and democracy in Latin America as well as in other parts of the world. And although the US economy is probably in a recession, Germany, Japan, and the EC after the completion of the Single European Market (SEM), are likely to continue to grow, averting a general global recession such as the one the world experienced in the early 1980s.

The prospects would seem to be reasonably good for the Latin American countries to at last benefit from expanding world trade, but the surprising conclusion of Wolf Grabendorff's paper is that they are not likely to do so. He concludes that the effects of the SEM "on Latin America—both positive and negative—will be somewhat marginal" and that even Latin America's traditional exports to the US market are not likely to grow in 1988-95 at more than the relatively slow rate that dominated the years 1980-88.

What is one to make of these conclusions? Grabendorff may well be right. Considering the continued deadlock in the Uruguay Round, no one seems to be particularly impressed these days by the possible gains from more liberal trade. Respected economists, in fact, are telling us that the costs of increasing protectionism are likely to be quite manageable.

I have enough doubt about this general "export pessimism," however, to raise a few questions. The questions are intended to provoke additional discussion, not to criticize a paper that provides an excellent departure point for our discussion.

## Critical Questions

First, much depends on how the benefits of agricultural liberalization are assessed. Grabendorff notes that the benefits for producers and consumers in Latin America would vary, but that the "net income effect would still be positive." According to some studies, however, this net effect could be quite substantial.[1] In 1995, it could amount to some $8 billion per year for Latin American countries, compared with a net income loss in Africa and Asia of $12 billion and $9 billion per year respectively. This assumes that only industrial countries liberalize their agricultural policies. If developing countries did so as well, the benefits for Latin America could total $13.4 billion per year by 1995. None of this includes the liberalization of tropical agricultural products, which would further benefit Latin American countries such as Brazil and Colombia.

Second, agricultural protection in Europe is a contributing constraint on industrial imports from Latin American and other developing countries. Grabendorff notes that EC imports from Latin America are skewed more toward primary products than EC imports from the world as a whole (three-quarters of Latin American exports to the EC compared to two-thirds to the world). Net economic welfare effects in the EC from agricultural liberalization would amount to $22 billion per year by 1995.[2] (Similar effects would occur in Japan). Cumulatively, these effects could be two-thirds or so as large as the expected efficiency benefits of the SEM.[3] Admittedly, much of this additional demand in the EC may be absorbed by trade diversion to industrial country suppliers, or additional imports from the developing Asian countries that have been displacing Latin American exporters in EC markets, but this need not be the case, especially if Latin American exporters anticipate this substantial new market for industrial products.

Grabendorff concludes that SEM will have only marginal effects on Latin America because EC trade with Latin America is less concerned with manufactured goods. He doesn't explain, however, why EC trade is less concerned with manufactured goods. It is so, in part, because agricultural protection is not only a direct constraint on Latin America's agricultural exports to the EC but an indirect constraint on Latin America's industrial exports to the EC.

Third, Latin America's inability to exploit growing export markets for manufactured goods in either the EC or the United States has been a function of the internal policies of Latin American countries. These are now changing. Is it not possible that Latin American exporters could become more competitive with Asian rivals in the 1990s, especially if the EC, Japan, and the United States make concerted efforts to encourage trade liberalization with developing countries? In the early and mid-1980s, many Latin American countries pursued adjustment policies that imposed even greater obstacles on their manufactured exports. While they continued to pursue inflationary domestic policies, they devalued their currencies, sharply increased import barriers, and substantially increased export subsidies. They achieved improved trade balances, i.e., a surplus of exports over imports with which to pay off external debt, but at an exorbitantly high cost.[4]

Today, the policy trends are totally different. Mexico, Chile, Colombia, and Venezuela were the first to adopt more market-oriented domestic policies and more liberal trade policies. Today, Brazil, Argentina, and even Peru are struggling to move in this direction. For the first time in the postwar period, Latin American countries are trying to give markets and freer trade a chance.

But now they are confronted by "export pessimism" in the industrial countries. The failure of the Uruguay Round makes it the first postwar trade round to end in disagreement. Even if the negotiations are revived, they will certainly not go anywhere very fast. To be sure, the United States has launched a new "Enterprise for the Americas" initiative, calling for, among other things, bilateral free trade agreements with Latin American countries. Bilateral trade, however, offers much less compared to multilateral trade, and free trade agreements in the Western Hemisphere, along with Grabendorff's prediction that SEM won't matter much for Latin American countries, will do very little to alter the pattern of heavy Latin American dependence on the US market and declining dependence on the EC or Japanese market.

Fourth, the data I have assembled in Table 1 suggest, at first glance, that the EC and particularly its expansion in 1973 to include the United Kingdom (and Denmark and Ireland) and in 1986 to include Spain and Portugal have been associated with a general decline in the significance of the EC markets for the exports of principal Latin American countries. In my judgment, the problem probably has less to do with the process and expansion of European integration per se than the general health of the world trading system in which EC integration takes place. As the world trading system comes under greater stress and threatens, in the wake of the Uruguay Round collapse, to dissolve into regional blocs, EC integration becomes a greater obstacle to Latin American exports.

Table 1 shows that, in the late 1960s when the world trading system was moving forward with the conclusion of the Kennedy Round, the principal Latin American countries exported a substantial (30-55 percent) and in most cases (excepting Mexico and Venezuela) rising share of their total exports to the EC-twelve countries (only six of which were members of the EC at the time). In the 1970s and 1980s, when the trading system came under increasing stress, these shares generally declined. They went down sharply in the 1970s for Argentina, Brazil, Chile, and Peru and continued down in the 1980s for Brazil and Chile, while evening out for Argentina and rising significantly for Peru (the only exception in the 1980s). While these shares went up significantly in the 1970s for Mexico, Venezuela, and Colombia, they went down for these same countries in the 1980s. By 1988 the share of exports going to the EC was below 1970 levels for Venezuela and Colombia and only slightly above 1966 levels in the case of Mexico.

The table breaks out the share of exports from the principal Latin American countries going to the three largest European countries joining the EC after 1970. The share going to the United Kingdom is down after 1970 (the last year shown before UK entry) for all countries except Peru. (It rises and then falls for Mexico.) The share going to Spain is also down after 1985 (last year shown before Spanish entry) for all countries except Chile and Peru. Only the share going to Portugal, which is the smallest in absolute terms, goes up or stays the same after 1985 (last year shown before Portuguese entry). While these generally downward trends cannot be attributed to the expansion of the EC (the trend was downward in many but not all cases before EC entry), it is at least safe to conclude that the EC and its enlargement have not been a positive factor enhancing the importance of EC markets for Latin American exports.

So Grabendorff's conclusions about the impact of EC market developments on Latin American trade are not wrong; they just don't say very much about the reasons why this impact may be minimal. It may be minimal, according to this brief critique, for four reasons, all of which the EC could do something about if it chose to. First, the Common Agricultural Policy (CAP) imposes significant net welfare costs on Latin American agricultural producers (including exporters) and consumers (including importers). Second, the CAP also depresses aggregate demand for manufactured goods in EC markets and hence indirectly restricts import demand for Latin American industrial exports. Third, the EC has not taken a significant initiative to encourage liberal trade and other economic reforms in Latin America (either bilaterally, as in the case of the US Enterprise for the Americas Initiative, or multilaterally in the Uruguay Round).

Finally, the expansion of the EC has done little to enhance the importance of EC markets for Latin American exports. Indeed, it may have potentially negative effects in the future, for as the EC expands it may possibly come to include Central European markets—with which Latin American countries conduct little trade—and Eastern European countries—whose commodity and agricultural exports compete directly with those of Latin American countries.

# Notes

1. John Whaley, ed., *Rules, Power and Credibility*, vol. I, *Thematic Studies from a Ford Foundation Project on Developing Countries and the Global Trading System* (London, Ontario: Centre for the Study of International Economic Relations, The University of Western Ontario, 1988), 168-71.

2. Ibid.

3. Over six years, the SEM was estimated to increase welfare 5-6 percent of gross domestic product (GDP). The $20 billion per year welfare effect of agricultural liberalization amounts to about 3-4 percent of GDP over six years.

4. See my recent book, *The Myth of America's Decline: Leading the World Economy into the 1990s* (New York: Oxford University Press, 1990), 285-9; and my article "The NICS in a New Trade Round," in *Hard Bargaining Ahead: U.S. Trade Policy and Developing Countries*, ed. Ernest H. Preeg (New Brunswick, N.J.: Transaction Books, 1985), 63-85.

# 3

# Latin American Trade Relations with Japan: New Opportunities in the 1990s?

*Barbara Stallings*

Latin America's interest in Japan increased substantially during the 1980s. Unfortunately for the region, however, Japan's priorities have moved in the opposite direction—toward the advanced industrial countries, especially the United States and booming Asia. Although the Latin American share of Japan's economic transactions has fallen, the absolute value has stayed constant or even increased, thus providing significant help in the face of an otherwise depressing international picture. In addition, there are specific examples of Latin American countries that have succeeded in stepping up their Japanese relations, both in trade and foreign investment.

In view of the topic of the conference, this chapter will focus on Latin America's trade with Japan. It should be recognized, however, that trade has been the lagging sector in Japan's economic relations with the region. As will be discussed in more detail later on, trade relations have centered on Japanese exports of industrial goods to Latin America in exchange for raw materials. Although accounting for more than 9 percent of Japanese trade in the 1950s, that figure dropped to less than 4 percent during the last half of the 1980s. Unlike the well-known situation with the United States, where Japan's economic interactions are trade-dominated, Japan's relations with Latin America have been investment and finance-dominated. This disparity will be analyzed in the following section, which puts trade within the overall context of Japanese-Latin American economic relations. The second and third sections will look at quantitative trends with respect to trade and some "special features" of Japanese trade (the general trading companies or *sogo shosha*, the links between trade and investment, and governmental attempts to promote trade). The fourth section will briefly compare US-Latin American trade with the data already presented for Japan. Finally, the chapter will outline three possible scenarios for the future of trilateral US-Japanese-Latin American trade and economic interactions.

## Japanese Economic Relations with Latin America

Japan's initial relations with Latin America came through immigration.[1] Beginning in the last quarter of the nineteenth century, more than three hundred thousand Japanese citizens migrated to Latin America. It is now estimated that more than one million people of Japanese descent live in the region. While most are in Brazil, other countries such as Mexico, Peru, and Paraguay also have substantial Japanese populations. It is generally thought that the large group of Japanese descendents in Brazil was one reason for Japan's strong economic interest in that country in the post-World War II period. A more recent demonstration of interest in Latin Americans of Japanese ancestry was the publicity surrounding the election of Alberto Fujimori as president of Peru and the ensuing possibility of large-scale aid to that country.

In more conventional economic terms, Japan has developed in the last thirty years multifaceted relations with Latin America. These include trade, direct investment, and both public and private financing. Currently, Japan has some $32 billion of direct foreign investment (DFI) in the region, which represents 17 percent of Japanese DFI worldwide.[2] While this figure has remained more or less constant for several decades, the 1980s have seen an important—and negative—change in the composition of both US and Japanese investment in Latin America. Two parallel processes have been occurring.

On the one hand, investment has shifted away from mainland Latin America toward the tax havens of the Caribbean islands and the flag-of-convenience companies in Panama. On the other hand, there has been a move away from the productive sectors toward services. In the 1970s, for example, 46 percent of Japanese DFI was in manufacturing (mainly in Brazil and Mexico). Another 30 percent was in agriculture, fishing, mining, and construction. Only 24 percent was in services (including finance and transportation). By the second half of the 1980s, those figures had changed dramatically. Manufacturing was down to 6.5 percent and other productive sectors had dropped to 1.4 percent. Services had ballooned to 92 percent. The latter was due mainly to flag-of-convenience shipping in Panama and offshore financial services in the Caribbean. If we eliminate these two categories, Japanese direct investment stock in Latin America drops to around $10 billion or only 5 percent of worldwide Japanese DFI.

Of this $10 billion of "real" investment, more than half is in Brazil with iron ore and steel as the single largest investment, followed by machinery and textiles. Mexico is the second major site of "real" Japanese DFI in Latin America. There, the automobile industry is the key sector, followed by mining and steel. Despite the recent years of devastation, Peru's mining sector still retains significant Japanese capital. It should be added that several promising investments emerged in 1990. New capital was injected into Chile's copper mining and into its paper/forestry sector. New investments will also be made in aluminum production in Brazil and Venezuela, and in the automobile industry in Mexico and perhaps Brazil. Whether these announcements are the beginning of a new confidence in Latin America on the part of the Japanese remains to be seen.

The other area where Japan is a major presence is with respect to Latin America's foreign debt. By some measures, Japan is now the leading creditor for the region as far as medium and long-term private bank loans are concerned. Official Japanese statistics for 1989 show that Japanese banks held $46 billion of Latin American debt, which represents 18 percent of total Japanese bank loans, down from 31 percent in the early 1980s.[3] While US government data show that US banks hold $36 billion of Latin American loans, differences in accounting procedures make these figures difficult to compare. Nonetheless, if Japan is not Latin America's largest creditor, it is certainly the second largest. While US banks have been withdrawing from the Latin American market since the debt crisis began in 1982, despite attempts by the International Monetary Fund and the Federal Reserve to keep all banks involved in the rescheduling negotiations, the Japanese banks have continued to participate. Thus, the decreasing US involvement in the region has caused a dramatic increase of Japan's share of the Latin American financial market. This trend seems to have been reversed during 1990, however, with the implementation of the Brady Plan for Mexico and Venezuela. The Japanese banks have elected to take writedowns on their loans rather than provide new money to those countries. The implication is that they, too, want out of the Latin American market.

In addition to private finance, the Japanese have also provided important public-sector credits to Latin America, both directly (through bilateral arrangements) and indirectly (through contributions to the multilateral agencies, including the Inter-American Development Bank). Japanese public funds are distributed through three main agencies. The first channel is through the Ministry of Foreign Affairs and the Japanese International Cooperation Agency (JICA), which dispense grants and technical assistance. Although by definition, there is no outstanding debt through this source, an idea of its importance can be seen by the latest annual figures. For 1988, Latin America received about $280 million in these two categories, accounting for 6.5 percent of total grant aid and 13 percent of the total technical cooperation.[4]

The second channel for public monies is the Overseas Economic Cooperation Fund (OECF), which distributes soft loans to developing countries. The interest rate on the loans is 2.6 percent with a maturity of twenty-eight years. As of March 31, 1990, Latin America had loans outstanding to OECF for $1.4 billion, representing about 4 percent of the total.[5] Typically, the region has not been eligible for much money from this source since it is aimed at the poorest countries, the current per capita income ceiling being $2,200. Although arrears must first be cleared, OECF officials say that they intend to increase, in the coming years, Latin America's share of funds as well as the absolute amount. This source will become increasingly important since Japan has now displaced the United States as the leading supplier of Official Development Assistance (ODA) and will distribute some $50 billion over the next five years.

The biggest source of public funds for Latin America is the Export-Import Bank of Japan (JEXIM). Like its sister organizations in the United States and Europe, JEXIM began in order to promote Japanese exports. Its most important function today, however, is to provide "untied direct loans" to governments of middle-income developing countries at rates similar to those of the World Bank. Latin America's $6.9 billion loans outstanding to JEXIM represent 19 percent of its total loans.[6] If we combine the OECF and JEXIM funds, Latin America accounts for about 10 percent of the debt owed to the Japanese public sector.

JEXIM and OECF are also the two organizations responsible for disbursing loans under Japan's "recycling fund," of which Latin America has become a leading recipient. This fund, now in its second phase, will provide $65 billion by its conclusion in 1992. A substantial part will go directly to the international financial institutions, but JEXIM will distribute $23.5 billion and OECF $12.5 billion, through co-financing and direct loans. As of mid-1990, JEXIM had committed 29 percent of its loans to Latin America and OECF 16 percent.[7] The preceding discussion has concerned *stocks* of Japanese capital in Latin America: 17 percent of Japanese direct investment (5 percent of non-financial/flag-of-convenience investment), 18 percent of total private bank debt, and 10 percent of public-sector debt are located in Latin America. These numbers contrast sharply with the trade figures since Latin America accounts for about 4 percent of Japanese total trade. If we look at *flows* over the past five years, rather than stocks, some similar results emerge (see Table 1). In general, over that period, Latin America has become less important to Japan, displaced by the United States, Southeast Asia, and increasingly Europe. Conversely, Japan has become more important to Latin America as other sources of capital have dried up. In particular, Table 1 suggests that Japan has provided about $9 billion per year on a net basis, while the United States has provided only $5 billion.

## Japanese Trade with Latin America

Trade between Japan and Latin America has never been of major importance for either side, but it has provided each partner with an avenue to diversify trade relations so as to be less dependent on its principal markets and suppliers. According to Japanese figures, total trade with Latin America (exports plus imports) was running at about $17.5 billion in 1989, representing 3.6 percent of Japan's total trade.[8] After peaking to more than 9.5 percent of Japan's total exports and imports in the mid-1950s, Latin America's share of Japanese trade has been consistently decreasing (see Table 2). Despite the falling share, however, the nominal value climbed rapidly until the early 1980s where it has stagnated. Only in 1988 did the total value of trade exceed the previous peak in 1981. Of course, the real value remains well below the 1981 level.

The balance of trade between Japan and Latin America has shifted over the period. During the 1950s and 1960s, Japan was running a small deficit as its import demand exceeded the goods it was able to sell in the region. Since the early 1970s, Japanese imports have increased, but not as fast as exports. Initially, the resulting imbalance was owed to the availability of borrowed resources in Latin America, but the pattern continued even after the debt crisis began in 1982. Up until 1987, the Japanese surplus was running at about $2 billion per year. As of 1989, it

## Table 1. US and Japanese Economic Transactions with the World, 1985-89

(annual averages, billions of dollars)

| Type of Flow | United States | | Japan | |
|---|---|---|---|---|
| **Trade**[a] | | | | |
| Advanced Industrial Nations | $434.2 | (63.7%) | $215.4 | (56.5%) |
| Third World | 247.9 | (36.3) | 165.6 | (43.5) |
|     Latin America | 88.9 | (13.0) | 15.2 | (4.0) |
|     Asia | 119.1 | (17.5) | 111.0 | (29.1) |
|     Africa | 16.7 | (2.4) | 7.6 | (2.0) |
|     Middle East | 23.2 | (3.4) | 31.8 | (8.3) |
| Total | 682.1 | (100.0) | 381.0 | (100.0) |
| **Private Bank Loans**[b] | | | | |
| Advanced Industrial Nations | -2.4 | (n.a.) | 25.4 | (69.2) |
| Third World | -4.6 | (n.a.) | 10.8 | (29.8) |
|     Latin America | -2.5 | (n.a.) | 4.4 | (12.2) |
|     Asia | -1.5 | (n.a.) | 5.7 | (15.7) |
|     Africa | -0.3 | (n.a.) | 0.6 | (1.6) |
|     Middle East | -0.3 | (n.a.) | 0.1 | (0.3) |
| Total | -7.0 | (n.a.) | 36.2 | (100.0) |
| **Direct Foreign Investment** | | | | |
| Advanced Industrial Nations | 22.0 | (76.7) | 20.1 | (70.0) |
| Third World | 6.7 | (23.3) | 8.6 | (30.0) |
|     Latin America | 6.0 | (20.9) | 4.6 | (16.0) |
|     Asia | 1.0 | (3.5) | 3.5 | (12.2) |
|     Africa | -0.1 | (—) | 0.4 | (1.4) |
|     Middle East | -0.1 | (—) | 0.1 | (0.3) |
| Total | 28.7 | (100.7) | 28.7 | (100.0) |
| **Development Aid**[c] | | | | |
| Third World | 7.4 | (100.0) | 4.5 | (100.0) |
|     Latin America | 1.6 | (22.2) | 0.3 | (7.4) |
|     Asia | 1.4 | (19.4) | 3.3 | (72.6) |
|     Africa | 1.0 | (13.5) | 0.5 | (11.2) |
|     Middle East | 3.3 | (44.9) | 0.4 | (8.8) |

[a]Exports plus imports.
[b]Medium and long-term loans.
[c]ODA only.

Sources: IMF, *Direction of Trade Statistics* (US and Japanese trade); OECD, *Development Cooperation* (US and Japanese trade); *Country Exposure Lending Survey* (US bank loans); Finance Ministry, *Annual Report of International Finance Bureau* (Japanese bank loans); Survey of Current Business (US direct investment); JEI Report 31A, August 11, 1989 (Japanese direct investment).

## Table 2.  Japanese Trade with Latin America, 1950-89

(millions of dollars)

| Year | Export Value | Percent* | Import Value | Percent* |
|------|------|------|------|------|
| 1950 | $47.1 | 5.7 | $67.1 | 6.9 |
| 1955 | 185.6 | 9.2 | 243.4 | 9.8 |
| 1960 | 298.3 | 7.4 | 309.6 | 6.9 |
| 1965 | 457.9 | 5.4 | 707.9 | 8.7 |
| 1970 | 1,112.2 | 5.8 | 1,368.7 | 7.2 |
| 1975 | 4,667.0 | 8.4 | 2,510.0 | 4.3 |
| 1980 | 8,572.0 | 6.6 | 5,702.0 | 4.0 |
| 1981 | 10,119.0 | 6.7 | 6,595.0 | 4.6 |
| 1982 | 8,726.0 | 6.3 | 6,201.0 | 4.7 |
| 1983 | 5,902.0 | 4.0 | 6,368.0 | 5.0 |
| 1984 | 7,899.0 | 4.7 | 7,097.0 | 5.2 |
| 1985 | 7,753.0 | 4.4 | 6,188.0 | 4.7 |
| 1986 | 8,716.0 | 4.1 | 6,087.0 | 4.8 |
| 1987 | 8,151.0 | 3.5 | 6,221.0 | 4.1 |
| 1988 | 8,673.0 | 3.3 | 8,198.0 | 4.4 |
| 1989 | 8,837.0 | 3.2 | 8,639.0 | 4.1 |

*Percent of total (worldwide) Japanese exports/imports.

Source: IMF, *Direction of Trade Statistics Yearbook*, various issues.

has fallen to less than $300 million, mainly because of an increase in Latin American exports (see Table 2).

The trade figures, and their country distribution within Latin America, are confused by Japan's relations with Panama. Since the mid-1970s, Japan has been using Panama as an important registry for its shipping fleet. Thus, sales of ships to Japanese companies in Panama have inflated trade figures for Latin America by a substantial amount. During the 1980s, Japanese data (also used by international organizations) show Panama as the recipient of $26.4 billion of Japanese exports or 34 percent of the Latin American total. The Panamanian figures, by contrast, do not include the shipping exports, since they have little or nothing to do with the Panamanian economy. These exports to Panama also distort the trade balance calculations since there is no corresponding inflation of imports. Without the very large surplus in Panama, Japanese trade with Latin America is in deficit.[9]

Aside from Panama, Japan's largest trade partner in Latin America has been Brazil. In 1989, Brazilian trade was 25 percent of Japan's total involvement in the region (or 29 percent if the Panamanian ships are excluded). Typically, Brazil has had a large surplus in its Japanese trade balance. Mexico is second with 21 percent of Japan's Latin American trade. The balance of Japanese-Mexican trade in the 1980s depended heavily on the price of oil. In 1988-89, Mexico had a small deficit with Japan. The third largest partner is Chile with 11 percent of Japan's Latin American trade, again with a large surplus in Chile's favor. Others, in order of importance, include Colombia (4.5%), Venezuela (4.3%), Argentina (3.4%), Peru (3.3%), Ecuador (1.3%), and Honduras (1.1%).

The content of Japanese-Latin American trade has been and remains a typical "colonial" pattern. Japan imports raw materials from Latin America and exports industrial goods in return. While US trade with Latin America has shifted away from this pattern, as will be discussed below, Japanese trade has not changed very much. A superficial look at Table 3 may give a mistaken impression of the nature of Latin American exports to Japan. While it appears that 41 percent of Japanese imports from the region are "manufactured goods," this figure includes not only finished goods but also what have traditionally been called "semi-manufactured goods." Thus, a closer look shows that about three-quarters of these "manufactured goods" are in fact semi-processed metals.

Turning to look at trade patterns in more detail, Table 3 shows the main categories as of 1989. Some 92 percent of Japanese exports to Latin America are "heavy and chemical industry" products. Of that amount, the largest share (46 percent of the total) is transport equipment. Once again the shipping trade with Panama creates confusion since more than half of the transport category is comprised of ships. Aside from that, general machinery, electrical instruments, and motor vehicles are the most important items.

Imports from Latin America are more varied. Foodstuffs account for 20 percent, with coffee as the largest single item. Raw materials are 26 percent (mostly iron ore) and petroleum is another 12 percent. As mentioned above, "manufactured goods" appear as the largest category. Breaking this down, however, shows that machinery and textiles provide 3 percent and steel another 9 percent while the remainder is mostly semi-processed metals. Exporters of "true" manufactured goods, rather than semi-manufactured materials, are mainly Brazil, Mexico, Argentina, and Venezuela. In general, however, Latin American countries have had little success in competing with Asia for the growing Japanese market for manufactured products.

Table 3.   Japanese Trade with Latin America by Sector, 1989

| Goods | Value | Percent |
|---|---|---|
| *Exports from Japan* | $9,380.8 | 100.0 |
| Foodstuffs | 41.5 | 0.4 |
| Raw Materials and Fuels | 74.1 | 0.8 |
| Light Industrial Goods | 525.5 | 5.6 |
| Textiles | (75.5) | (0.8) |
| Other | (450.0) | (4.8) |
| Heavy Industrial Goods | 8,641.7 | 92.1 |
| Chemical Goods | (227.0) | (3.0) |
| Metal Goods | (580.1) | (6.2) |
| Machinery | (7,784.5) | (83.0) |
| General | [1,257.7] | [13.0] |
| Electrical | [1,940.4] | [20.7] |
| Transportation | [4,299.1] | [45.8] |
| Precision Instruments | [287.3] | [3.1] |
| Non-classified | 98.1 | 1.0 |
| | | |
| *Imports to Japan* | 8,870.6 | 100.0 |
| Foodstuffs | 1,761.2 | 19.9 |
| Raw Materials | 2,335.4 | 26.3 |
| Textile Materials | (138.9) | (1.6) |
| Metallic Materials | (1,446.2) | (16.3) |
| Others | (750.3) | (8.5) |
| Mineral Fuels | 1,055.1 | 11.9 |
| Manufactured Goods | 3,657.4 | 41.2 |
| Chemicals | (573.1) | (6.5) |
| Machinery | (223.8) | (2.5) |
| Metal Goods | (2,477.7) | (27.9) |
| Iron and Steel | [834.2] | [9.4] |
| Nonferrous Metals | [1,638.5] | [18.5] |
| Others | (382.8) | (4.3) |
| Non-classified | 61.6 | 0.7 |

Source: MITI, *White Paper on International Trade*, Japan 1990.

Despite Latin America's low overall share of Japan's market, there are some specific items where the region is an important supplier. According to unpublished data provided by the Ministry of International Trade and Industry (MITI), Latin America provides at least 20 percent of Japan's imports of seven food products as well as a number of raw materials. The largest items include iron ore ($960 million, 30% of Japanese imports), coffee ($587 million, 66%), unwrought copper ($574 million, 34%), ferroalloys ($285 million, 23%), silver ($174 million, 76%), pig iron ($128 million, 36%), emeralds ($102 million, 28%), forage ($101 million, 55%), and salt ($95 million, 46%).

Notwithstanding these isolated items, Latin America is not a very important trade partner for Japan. But how do things look from the Latin American side? For the nineteen traditionally defined Latin American countries, Japan accounted for a little more than 8 percent of their trade in 1989. In other words, Japan is about twice as important for them as they are for Japan. Furthermore, Japan is more significant as an export market (10 percent of Latin American exports are sold there) than as a provider of imports (less than 7 percent of imports originate in Japan).

For five Latin American countries Japan is the second largest export market after the United States. They include Chile (12.5% of exports are sold to Japan), Brazil (12.2%), Peru (11.9%), Honduras (9.8%), and Mexico (7.1%). For Colombia, Japan is the third most important market (5.2%). Similarly for imports, Japan is the second largest provider, again following the United States, for Ecuador (13.9%), Colombia (10.9%), Panama (10.6%), Honduras (9.0%), Haiti (5.4%), and Mexico (5.3%). For five others, Japan is third most important: Dominican Republic (14.4%), Paraguay (13.0%), Chile (7.7%), Costa Rica (6.7%), and Brazil (6.6%). All data are for 1989.[10]

Chile has made a particular effort to increase its exports to Japan, and has had significant success. For example, between 1986 and 1989 Chilean exports to Japan increased by 150 percent from $533 million to $1.3 billion. Copper's share has been falling, despite the high world prices, which means that non-traditional goods—especially fish, fruits, and forestry products—have been growing rapidly. Mexico also has been trying to increase non-traditional exports. In the last year alone, non-oil exports to Japan have increased by 14 percent.[11]

## Special Features of Japanese Trade

Three special features are found in Japanese trade with Latin America. First is the role of the trading companies. Second is the close link between trade and investment, in which the trading companies are heavily involved. And third is the important role of the government in promoting trade.

Behind the quantitative data on Japanese-Latin American trade lies a fascinating story about the trade process. The key actors are the giant general trading companies or *sogo shosha*, which are among the most powerful companies in Japan.[12] Some of the *sogo shosha* date back to the last century and were central figures in the *zaibatsu* (conglomerates), which led Japan's dramatic industrialization drive in the late nineteenth and early twentieth centuries. The most powerful *sogo shosha*, like the *zaibatsu* themselves, were broken up during the postwar US occupation. By the 1950s, however, a shift in US opinion encouraged the trading companies to regroup. After various mergers and divisions, there are now generally considered to be nine *sogo shosha* at the top of a trading sector including hundreds of smaller, more specialized firms. The nine companies are huge. Their trading transactions in the 1989 fiscal year ranged from $35 billion (*Kanematsu*) to $143 billion (*Sumitomo*). The six largest have an average of 150 international offices in more than eighty countries in addition to fifty or so offices in Japan.

The general trading companies have three principal functions. First is the obvious role of intermediary. The companies purchase goods of all kinds ("noodles to missiles" in the popular parlance) and sell them to clients, primarily in Japan but also in third countries. In the process, they may transport and warehouse these goods. Second, they act as bankers. Much of the short-term trade credit is provided by the *sogo shosha* themselves. As will be discussed below, they also provide significant amounts of equity capital to secure suppliers. Finally, the trading companies gather social, political, and economic information. Some say this information is far superior to that of the Japanese government itself. Large amounts of money are now being devoted to improve communication equipment to process and transmit this information through the trading companies' vast international networks.[13]

Although the *sogo shosha* were involved in international trade almost since the beginning, most of their initial efforts focused on the needs of the Japanese market. Thus, their primary activity involved purchasing raw materials abroad and selling the output, both abroad and at home. In the 1970s, however, large Japanese companies began to develop their own sales operations and financing, which led many economists to predict that the trading companies would disappear. Instead, they transferred more of their operations abroad, especially to Third World countries and in the process increasingly became organizers of projects as well as sales agents.

Several of the *sogo shosha* set up offices in Latin America before World War II, but it was really in the postwar period that they became major actors in the region. Since the larger companies tend to move in tandem, it is possible to trace waves of movement into Latin America. In the 1950s, the trading companies established subsidiaries in Brazil, Argentina, and Mexico. In the 1960s, they entered Chile, Peru, and Venezuela. Colombia and Panama followed in the 1970s, and Ecuador came in the 1980s. Many other countries have representatives or liaison offices, which cannot formally sign contracts or accumulate profits, but are nevertheless important as part of the international network of the firms. Indeed, the international span of operations is one of the key characteristics of the *sogo shosha*. Table 4 shows the location of trading company offices in Latin America. As can be seen, six of the nine companies have offices in thirteen or fourteen Latin American countries, while the smaller ones cover from five to nine countries.

Trading remains the dominant activity of the *sogo shosha* in Latin America. The largest companies engage in an average of $2-3 billion in yearly transactions (which represents perhaps 2 percent of their total transactions, although 10 percent of their offices are in the region). In a typical situation, one-third of that amount is exports from Japan, another third is imports to Japan, and the final third is offshore or third-country trade. This means that more than half of the yearly $18 billion of Japanese-Latin American trade is handled by the nine *sogo shosha*. More surprising is that perhaps 10 percent of total Latin American trade (about $200 billion per year) is handled by these same firms.[14]

The *sogo shosha* are crucial in three areas: exports of non-traditional goods to Japan, third-country trade in general, and investment in products that are then exported. The *sogo shosha* have been particularly important for small and medium-sized firms—both in helping such Japanese firms to operate abroad and helping foreign firms trade with Japan. The Mexican government, for example, says that the trading companies handle almost all exports of Mexican manufactured goods. Chilean fruits, seafood, and forestry products are exported by the *sogo shosha*. Likewise, the traders promote exports of machinery from Brazil, textiles from Central America, and many other new products.

During the 1980s, third-country trade became increasingly important for the *sogo shosha* in Latin America. As the domestic market slowed

Table 4.  Japanese Trading Company Offices[a] in Latin America by Country, 1990

| Country | MI | MB | SU | MA | CI | NI | KA | NC | TO |
|---|---|---|---|---|---|---|---|---|---|
| Mexico | 3 | 2 | 2 | 2 | 1 | 3 | 2 | 1 | 1 |
| Guatemala | 1 | 1 | 1 | 1 | 1 | 1 | 1 | 0 | 0 |
| El Salvador | 0 | 1 | 1 | 0 | 1 | 0 | 0 | 0 | 0 |
| Nicaragua | 1 | 0 | 0 | 0 | 0 | 0 | 0 | 0 | 0 |
| Costa Rica | 0 | 0 | 1 | 1 | 0 | 1 | 1 | 0 | 0 |
| Panama[b] | 1 | 1 | 1 | 0 | 1 | 1 | 0 | 1 | 1 |
| Cuba | 1 | 0 | 1 | 1 | 1 | 0 | 1 | 0 | 0 |
| Dominican Republic | 0 | 0 | 0 | 0 | 0 | 1 | 0 | 0 | 0 |
| Venezuela | 1 | 2 | 1 | 1 | 1 | 1 | 0 | 1 | 0 |
| Colombia | 1 | 1 | 1 | 1 | 2 | 1 | 0 | 0 | 0 |
| Ecuador | 2 | 1 | 1 | 1 | 1 | 1 | 0 | 0 | 2 |
| Bolivia | 0 | 1 | 0 | 1 | 1 | 1 | 0 | 0 | 0 |
| Peru | 1 | 1 | 1 | 1 | 1 | 1 | 1 | 1 | 1 |
| Chile | 1 | 1 | 1 | 1 | 1 | 1 | 1 | 0 | 0 |
| Paraguay | 1 | 1 | 0 | 1 | 1 | 1 | 1 | 0 | 0 |
| Argentina | 1 | 1 | 1 | 1 | 1 | 1 | 1 | 1 | 1 |
| Uruguay | 0 | 0 | 0 | 0 | 0 | 0 | 0 | 0 | 0 |
| Brazil | 6 | 7 | 7 | 5 | 3 | 3 | 2 | 2 | 3 |
| Number of offices[a] | 21 | 21 | 20 | 18 | 17 | 18 | 11 | 8 | 8 |
| Number of countries | 13 | 13 | 13 | 13 | 14 | 14 | 9 | 7 | 5 |

[a]Includes trading subsidiaries and representative/liaison offices.
[b]Several companies also have an "international" office in Panama.

| | | |
|---|---|---|
| MI=Mitsui | MA=Marubeni | KA=Kanematsu |
| MB=Mitsubishi | CI=C. Itoh | NC=Nichimen |
| SU=Sumitomo | NI=Nissho Iwai | TO=Toyo Menken |

Source: Annual reports.

down, especially for investment, fewer imports were required from Japan. It was also extremely difficult for Latin American goods other than raw materials to compete in the Japanese market. Thus, in its 1990 annual survey, the trading company C. Itoh reports that 45 percent of its Latin American business had now become third-country trade. Unpublished data from other *sogo shosha* suggest figures ranging up to one-third. Most of this trade is between Latin America and the United States, but goods are also shipped from Latin America to Asia and Europe. All of the trading firms declare that an increase in third-country trade is among their goals for the 1990s.

Finally, the *sogo shosha* are at the center of the link between trade and investment, which has always been a dominant characteristic of Japan's international activities. The traders themselves have become equity investors, often buying a small interest in firms offering good possibilities for export. Having such a share enables the trading companies to bring about changes that not only increase the firms' profitabilities but also improve their products, so as to make them more marketable abroad, including in Japan. While the trading companies usually hope to make profits from their investments, they are also interested in generating future trade opportunities.

There are two main types of Japanese-Latin American trade not handled by the *sogo shosha*. The major Japanese corporations with subsidiaries in Latin America generally export and import their own goods. This is an extension of the process that took place in Japan itself as manufacturing firms became increasingly independent of the trading companies. Similarly, large Latin American firms—especially state corporations—also deal directly with customers in Japan. Examples include *Petróleos Mexicanos* (PEMEX), which sells about $1 billion of oil each year to a Japanese consortium of refiners; *Companhia Vale do Rio Doce* (CVRD), the Brazilian firm that sells iron ore and other raw materials to Japan; *Corporación del Cobre* (CODELCO), which sells Chilean copper; and *Minería Peruana Comercial* (MINPECO) that distributes various Peruvian mineral products. In fact, of the large ticket raw materials that Latin America exports to Japan the trading companies only play a major role in the export of Colombian coffee and Mexican salt.

The Japanese government also plays a crucial role in international trade and investment. Perhaps the best known format is the so-called "national project." While there are many definitions of this term, its crucial aspect is the link between the public sector (usually through OECF) and private Japanese industry, together with the participation of a wide variety of private-sector Japanese firms. The trading companies often act as organizers of the projects. Important examples include three in Brazil (*Cerrado*, an agricultural complex that began in Minas Gerais; *Cenibra*, a paper and pulp project in the same region; and *Alunorte*, an aluminum project in Carajas). Two other steel projects are located in Mexico.

Another government role is to provide insurance for trade and investment through MITI. Like the participation of the OECF in the national projects, MITI insurance functions as a governmental approval or disapproval of particular projects and countries. Only very large firms or projects that are especially lucrative will go ahead without MITI insurance. Another way in which the government has stimulated trade in the past is through ODA. These ODA projects—often promoted by the trading companies themselves—generally revolve around the guarantee that the equipment needed for the project would be purchased from Japanese firms. More recently, the practice of tied loans has ended and the link between trade and ODA has weakened. Since Latin America gets very little Japanese ODA, this link is not very important. More relevant in the past, however, were JEXIM loans to promote Japanese exports, but these too have dried up in response to the friction caused by Japanese trade surplus. Now, JEXIM loans to Latin America are mostly untied. In general, the public-private links that spurred trade in the past are on the decline. This has softened private support for lending to developing countries.

## Comparisons between US and Japanese Trade with Latin America

Japan's trade with Latin America differs substantially from that of the United States. First and foremost, US trade in the region is much more important quantitatively to both the United States and Latin America. Equally different are the sectoral composition of US-Latin American trade and the trade process itself. For example, there is no US equivalent of the *sogo shosha* and the US government plays only a small role in the promotion of trade. Instead, links between trade and investment come through the multinational investors themselves.

Table 5 shows long-term trends in US-Latin American trade in the postwar period. Comparing it with Table 2 reveals two interesting points. The United States carries on much more of its trade with Latin America than does Japan. In 1989, 12.7 percent of US trade ($109 billion) was with Western Hemisphere countries compared to 3.7 percent for

Japan ($18 billion). Latin America was slightly more important as a market for US exports (13.5 percent of US exports) as it was a source of imports (12.2 percent of US imports). These differences are not at all surprising, however, given geographical and historical ties between the two markets.

More interesting, therefore, is the similarity in the two tables: the declining importance of Latin America for both countries. In fact, the timing pattern is also very similar. In both cases, the peak of Latin American participation was in the 1950s. There has been a fairly steady decline ever since, with a more pronounced downward shift in the late 1980s. These trends, of course, are matched in other areas. Two decades ago, Aníbal Pinto was already writing about the increasing marginalization of Latin America.[15] The trade component of this marginalization is consistent with the import-substitution development strategy followed by Latin America and the "export pessimism" that accompanied it. Since the Asian countries were promoting trade—or at least exports—at the same time, they eventually overtook Latin America in share of world trade. The four East Asian newly industrializing countries (Korea, Tai-

**Table 5. US Trade with Latin America, 1950-89**

| Year | Export Value | Percent* | Import Value | Percent* |
|------|------|------|------|------|
| 1950 | $2.8 | 27.2 | $3.1 | 34.8 |
| 1955 | 3.5 | 22.4 | 3.6 | 31.6 |
| 1960 | 3.9 | 19.0 | 3.9 | 26.5 |
| 1965 | 4.3 | 15.6 | 4.4 | 20.6 |
| 1970 | 6.5 | 15.0 | 6.0 | 15.0 |
| 1975 | 17.1 | 15.8 | 16.2 | 16.4 |
| 1980 | 38.7 | 17.6 | 37.2 | 15.2 |
| 1981 | 41.9 | 17.6 | 40.8 | 14.9 |
| 1982 | 33.2 | 15.6 | 39.5 | 16.2 |
| 1983 | 25.3 | 12.9 | 43.5 | 16.1 |
| 1984 | 29.2 | 12.6 | 50.1 | 14.7 |
| 1985 | 30.3 | 13.8 | 49.2 | 13.3 |
| 1986 | 30.6 | 13.5 | 43.9 | 11.3 |
| 1987 | 34.4 | 13.6 | 49.0 | 11.6 |
| 1988 | 43.6 | 13.6 | 53.7 | 11.7 |
| 1989 | 49.1 | 13.5 | 60.1 | 12.2 |

*Percent of total (worldwide) US exports/imports.

Source: IMF, *Direction of Trade Statistics Yearbook*, various issues.

wan, Hong Kong, and Singapore) now supply a larger volume of US imports than do all Latin American countries combined.

The relative importance of individual Latin American nations provides another interesting contrast. Even leaving aside the anomalous situation of Panama, the differences remain significant. For Japan, Brazil is the most important trade partner as almost all of Japan's trade is with *South* America (with the exception of Mexico). For the United States, Mexico dominates the rest of the region. Mexico alone accounted for 48 percent of US trade with Latin America in 1989. Central America and the Caribbean account for another 15 percent, while giant Brazil, for example, represented only 13 percent. These geographical differences might provide the basis for complementary relations between the United States and Japan, or for increased friction. We will return to these issues in the concluding section.

The sectoral composition of trade is yet another area of contrast between Latin American economic relations with the United States and Japan. A couple of decades ago, the United States basically supplied industrial goods to Latin America in exchange for raw materials, much like the Japanese do today. That pattern, however, changed substantially during the 1980s. A comparison between Table 6 and Table 3 highlights these differences between the United States and Japan. First, raw materials from Latin America account for less than 4 percent of US imports while they compose more than a quarter of the Japanese imports from the region. Second, 27 percent of US imports consist of machinery compared to Japan's 2.5 percent. Finally, 11 percent of US imports are light manufactured goods as opposed to only 4 percent for Japan. Similar differences appear on the export side as Japan exports twice as much machinery to Latin America as the US. To some extent, of course, the trade differences between the United States and Japan are due to the greater natural resources of the former. The interesting question still remains: why has Latin America been so successful at exporting industrial goods to the United States while being almost completely shut out of the Japanese market, even for light manufactured products? The answer most often given in Japan is that Latin America has been unable to meet Japan's quality standards.

Finally, there are differences in the trade process that should be briefly mentioned. Clearly, there are no US equivalents to Japan's trading companies. The key intermediaries are the producing multinationals themselves. That is, intra-company trade is a major source of imports to

## Table 6. US Trade with Latin America by Sector, 1988

| Goods | Value | Percent |
|---|---|---|
| *Exports from US* | $43,749.7 | 100.0 |
| Foodstuffs | 3,846.2 | 8.8 |
| Raw Materials and Fuels | 4,369.1 | 10.0 |
| Light Industrial Goods | 4,077.9 | 9.3 |
| Heavy Industrial Goods | 29,575.8 | 67.6 |
|     Chemical Goods | (5,564.6) | (12.7) |
|     Metal Goods | (4,468.7) | (10.2) |
|     Machinery | (19,542.5) | (44.7) |
| Non-classified | 1,880.5 | 4.3 |
| | | |
| *Imports to US* | 51,271.8 | 100.0 |
| Foodstuffs | 8,631.9 | 16.8 |
| Raw Materials | 1,848.1 | 3.6 |
| Mineral Fuels | 11,154.4 | 21.8 |
| Manufactured Goods | 27,853.6 | 54.3 |
|     Chemicals | (1,694.6) | (3.3) |
|     Machinery | (13,791.0) | (26.9) |
|     Metal Goods | (6,394.0) | (12.5) |
|     Others | (5,744.0) | (11.2) |
| Non-classified | 1,783.8 | 3.5 |

Source: Department of Commerce, *US Foreign Trade Highlights*, 1988.

the United States from Latin America. Some of this is done in connection with special facilities set up in Central America and the Caribbean (the Caribbean Basin Initiative) and in Mexico (the *maquiladora* program). Japan has also been quick to take advantage of the latter. Figures vary, but probably about fifty Japanese firms have assembly plants along the Mexican border for export to the United States.[16]

Ironically, the US government is not actively promoting US exports to Latin America or elsewhere, despite the declared need to close the trade gap. Export-Import Bank loans have ground to a halt; likewise, the US Agency for International Development no longer stimulates trade except perhaps in Central America. Indeed, it is the Japanese government that is trying to stimulate US exports to Latin America! This is an open aim of the "recycling fund." The idea is that if Latin American countries have more foreign currency, they will use it to buy goods from the United States—and perhaps take some pressure off Japan. Whether true or not is open to question, but the combination is interesting to say the least.

## Scenarios for the Future

Moving from the past to the future, three main scenarios are being discussed with respect to trade between Japan, the United States, and Latin America. They include a Western Hemisphere trade bloc with little role for Japan; a Japanese "headquarters strategy" in which Japan displaces the United States, at least in South America; and some type of "cooperative" US-Japanese approach.

The extreme version of the trade bloc scenario, which has been under discussion for several years, envisions three major trade areas: Europe, East Asia, and the Americas. The Americas portion of that plan took a more concrete form with Mexican president Carlos Salinas's proposal for a US-Mexican Free Trade Area. Combined with the existing free trade agreement with Canada, this would provide a market of more than 300 million people. The Mexican proposal has been further expanded—although in an extremely vague way—by George Bush's Enterprise for the Americas Initiative. Since then, the United States has agreed to pursue free trade talks with several Latin American countries, but clearly the Mexican proposal is the most immediate. The future of trade with Latin America will depend largely on whether the US and Mexican congresses ratify the proposed free trade agreement and whether it will later be extended further south. In any case, even if such agreements are concluded, it is unclear what impact, if any, those external barriers will have on Japan and others.

While there is no better than a 50 percent chance that the Mexican agreement will be ratified, I will nevertheless concentrate my remarks on the potential impact that such an agreement would have on Japanese trade with both the United States and Latin America. Although Japan officially supports the Mexican agreement, the Japanese are privately suspicious that the intention, or at least the effect, will be to limit their participation in this new market. I have heard some off-the-record comments to this effect, but a *Wall Street Journal* article (November 13, 1990) made the position public. Japanese investors are fearful that the agreement will impose a stiff local content law for duty-free exports in either direction. It would also likely eliminate the possibility of duty-free imports of inputs that the *maquiladoras* now enjoy. According to the president of Nissan Mexicana, many Japanese would invest directly in the United States rather than in Mexico if confronted by such changes.

Nearly the opposite position has been put forward by Dr. Gabriel Szekely, an expert on Japanese-Mexican relations.[17] Szekely argues that the only way for Mexico to attract Japanese trade and investment is by establishing a free trade area with the United States. At the same time, he also claims that Japanese participation is a crucial factor to make an agreement work. Szekely's perspective shades off into the third (cooperative) scenario.

The exclusive version of the trade bloc theory seems highly unlikely, despite the recent collapse of the General Agreement on Tariffs and Trade (GATT) negotiations. An "Americas bloc" is simply not an attractive alternative for the United States. A slow-growing Latin American market, with a large share of the population cut off from consumption because of gross inequality in income distribution, is not sufficient compensation for losing access to the booming Asian markets. Even if stronger than expected protectionism emerges in Europe, a more likely response would be a very broad Pacific Basin strategy.

The second scenario, with Japan displacing the United States in Latin America, has been most forcefully advanced by Prof. Leon Hollerman.[18] Using Brazil as an example, Hollerman makes a twofold argument. First, he points out that the United States and Brazil are basically economic competitors, while Japan and Brazil have complementary economies. Moreover, the United States has alienated Brazil on many issues, while Japan is perceived as more cooperative. Second, Hollerman outlines a "headquarters" strategy, whereby Japan would increase its links with Brazil at the expense of the United States. In particular, Japan would take a multilateral approach, limiting its trade with the United States while helping Brazil to expand its US exports. The trading companies would play a key role in the process. "The ultimate implication for the United States is that instead of being *confronted* by Japan, it will be *outflanked* by Japan in accordance with the headquarters strategy."[19]

This scenario is also unlikely. My own interviews in Japan over the past three years find little interest in Latin America. Most of Japan's official activity in the region is to protect its relationship with the United States. As far as the private sector is concerned, I have met no one who expects a return to the level of activity of the 1970s. The banks have opted

out; non-financial investors are retaining their holdings but not expanding except in very special circumstances like Mexico's *maquiladoras* and
Chile's natural resources. Of course, the caveat should be added that if
growth and stability return, Japan will be present. Nonetheless, there is
little inclination to help bring about these goals. Hollerman is correct in
his focus on third-country trade, but it seems more a defensive strategy
than an offensive one.

The United States and Japan officially endorse the third scenario, that
of cooperation. Although what it involves is not exactly clear, the pre-
ferred US version would be for Japan to provide the money and for the
United States to spend it. Clearly, this approach would be unacceptable
to the Japanese over the long run although this is not unlike what has
been happening for the last several years. In the longer run, if Japan is
to continue to provide resources, it must also have a say in how they are
spent. When that comes about, conflicts are bound to emerge because
Japan's views on development and how to achieve it are different from
those of the United States. At the moment, the Japanese limit themselves
to expressing "puzzlement" over the US-approved strategies of liberalization and privatization that most Latin American governments have
adopted over the last several years. These strategies are very different
from the one that proved so successful for Japan and its neighbors in
East Asia.

The Japanese claim to be waiting for some serious indication of US
interest in Latin America. After all, Japan considers that Latin America
is in the US sphere of influence. If the United States takes the lead, they
will be willing to assist. The form and content remain to be clarified, and
a problem-free cooperative venture is unlikely.

# NOTES

1. For a summary discussion of immigration trends, see Iyo
Kunimoto, "Japanese Migration to Latin America," in *The United States,
Japan, and Latin America: A New Trilateralism in the Western Hemisphere?*,
ed. Barbara Stallings and Gabriel Szekely, forthcoming.

2. Data on direct foreign investment by Japan are kept by the Ministry
of Finance. Unfortunately, they consist of companies' *intentions* to invest,
as reported to the Ministry. No data on a regional basis exist for actual
investment. Likewise, data on reinvestment are not available. My assumption in using the data for "accumulated investment" is that those

investments that are declared but not actually made are more or less offset by reinvestment.

3. On debt and the role of the banks, see Barbara Stallings, "The Reluctant Giant: Japan and the Latin American Debt Crisis," *Journal of Latin American Studies* 22 (February 1990) and Kotaro Horisaka, "Japanese Banks and Latin American Debt Problems," *Latin American Studies Occasional Papers*, no. 4, Georgetown University, 1990.

4. Data are from the Ministry of Foreign Affairs, *ODA, Japan's Official Development Assistance, 1989 Report* (1990): 60.

5. Converted at Y158=$1. On OECF loans, see OECF, *Annual Report* (1990): 130.

6. Converted at Y158=$1. Export-Import Bank of Japan, *Annual Report* (1990): 24.

7. The best overall report on the recycling fund is Toshihiko Kinoshita, "Japan's Current 'Recycling Measures': Their Background, Performance, and Prospects," Export-Import Bank of Japan, October 1988. Updated information comes from unpublished data from JEXIM and OECF.

8. Trade data used here are from the IMF, *Direction of Trade Statistics Yearbook*, various years. They are based on Japanese government statistics; figures from the Latin American side vary, even in the same publication. The IMF figures for Japan's Western Hemisphere trade also differ slightly from those in the *MITI White Paper on International Trade, Japan 1990* (translation published by JETRO). The main difference concerns inclusion of countries; the MITI figures include areas that are not independent, of which the most important is Puerto Rico. The MITI data, used in the paper for sectoral analysis, show trade for 1989 of about $18 billion.

9. On the shipping trade and Panama's relations with Japan in general, see Charlotte Elton, "Japan and Panama: The Role of the Panama Canal," in Stallings and Szekely. Elton explains the link between the large investment and trade figures. Since the Japanese definition of direct investment includes loans, it is loans to the shipping companies (recorded as DFI) that finance the import of Japanese boats by Japanese companies in Panama.

10. Calculated from *Direction of Trade Statistics Yearbook* (1990).

11. Data provided by the Chilean and Mexican embassies in Tokyo.

12. Several analyses are available in English of the *sogo shosha*. The most useful is Kiyoshi Kojima and Terutomo Ozawa, *Japan's General Trading Companies: Merchants of Economic Development*, OECD, Paris, 1984. For more historical analysis, see also Yoshihara Kunio, *Sogo Shosha: The Vanguard of the Japanese Economy* (Oxford University Press, 1982).

13. These categories are listed in Kojima and Ozawa, but they are merely reporting what all economists and businesspeople in Japan say about the role of the trading companies.

14. Based on confidential interviews at the major trading companies.

15. Aníbal Pinto, "Economic Relations between Latin America and the United States: Some Implications and Perspectives," in *Latin America and the United States: The Changing Political Realities*, ed. Julio Cotler and Richard R. Fagen (Stanford University Press, 1974), 100-116.

16. Japanese External Trade Organization (JETRO), *Japanese Direct Foreign Investment* (in Japanese) (1990): 4.

17. Gabriel Szekely, "Japan, Mexico, and the United States: An Unusual Trilateral Relationship," in Stallings and Szekely.

18. Leon Hollerman, "The Role of Brazil in Japan's Economic Strategy: Implications for the United States" (Paper presented at the conference on Japan and Latin America, UCSD, April 1990). See also his book, *Japan's Economic Strategy in Brazil: Challenge for the United States* (Lexington Books, 1988).

19. Hollerman, "The Role of Brazil in Japan's Economic Strategy," 4.

# Japanese-Latin American Relations: A Different Perspective

*Tetsuro Iino*

In general, Barbara Stallings's chapter is informative, but because of our different experiences, my interpretation of the facts and figures is not the same.

First, it is important to compare the fundamental economic strength of Latin American countries over the past three decades with other regions of the world. By doing so, we can measure its health and potentiality for the future. We need to ask: what was Latin America's actual growth rate over the past three decades (see Table 1)?

During the 1960s, Latin America's economy grew at an average rate of 5.7 percent per year. During the 1970s, it continued to grow at the rate of 5.6 percent per year. But, surprisingly, its growth rate suddenly dropped to 1.4 percent during the seven years starting in 1980. In 1989 it slid further to 1.1 percent. It is worth noting that in the 1980s the modest economic strength of Latin America seems to have eroded substantially due to hyperinflation (Brazil, 1,765% in 1989; Argentina, 4,924% in 1989; and Nicaragua, 36,600% in 1988).

Table 2 shows a remarkable contrast with Asia: Asian newly industrializing countries and the "four tigers"—South Korea, Hong Kong, Formosa, and Singapore—achieved formidable economic growth with an average rate exceeding 8 percent per year every year for the last thirty without high inflation. During 1990, the previously mentioned "four tigers" expanded their economy at an annual growth rate of 6 percent.

What will happen to Latin America's share of world trade? Thirty years ago, its share of world export trade was about 8 percent. This share continued to decline to 6.5 percent in 1980 and then plummeted to 3.8 percent in 1987.

## Table 1.  Economic Growth of Selected Latin American Countries

(gross domestic product)

|  | 1960-70 | 1970-80 | 1980-86 |
|---|---|---|---|
| Mexico | 7.0 | 6.5 | 1.0 |
| Brazil | 6.1 | 8.7 | 2.9 |
| Argentina | 4.4 | 2.6 | -1.1 |
| Chile | 4.3 | 2.6 | 0.9 |
| Venezuela | 6.0 | 0.2 | -1.8 |
| Nicaragua | 7.0 | 0.5 | -1.9 |
| Peru | 5.0 | 3.9 | 1.3 |
| Panama | 7.9 | 5.4 | 2.6 |
| El Salvador | 5.6 | 3.0 | -1.4 |
| Costa Rica | 6.1 | 5.5 | 1.1 |
| Average of Latin America | 5.7 | 5.6 | 1.4 |

Source: Economic Commission for Latin America and the Caribbean.

## Table 2.  Economic Growth of Asia

(gross domestic product)

|  | 1960-70 | 1970-80 | 1980-90 (estimate) |
|---|---|---|---|
| NIES[a] Asia | 8.8 | 8.7 | 8.3 |
| ASEAN[b] | n.a. | 7.1 | 5.0 |
| China | 4.0 | 5.8 | 8.3 |
| Japan | 10.5 | 4.7 | 4.3 |

[a]South Korea, Taiwan, Singapore, Hong Kong.
[b]Philippines, Indonesia, Malaysia, Thailand.

Sources: *Gaiko Forum, Nikkei Shimbun* .

It was regrettable, indeed, that even Latin America's leading countries, such as Brazil, Mexico, and Argentina, suffered severe economic setbacks during the 1980s. This deterioration was presumably an aftereffect of their policy of continuous economic expansion in the 1970s—which depended too heavily on borrowing from overseas financial markets—compounded by Latin America's inability to cope with the oil crises of the 1970s, when the per barrel price of oil rose from $3 to $36. In addition, the political situation was aggravated by civil wars in Central America and by the spread of guerrilla and drug-related violence throughout the hemisphere.

These factors, taken with the accumulation of foreign debt and the resulting lack of real economic growth in the region are still casting a dark shadow over the future path of Latin America.

While it would appear, as Stallings asserts, that Japan's relationship with Latin America between 1985 and 1989 has been dominated by investment and finance, it is misleading to take as an article of faith that "trade with Latin America is becoming less and less important for Japan." First, despite the dramatic surge of Japanese capital (including official development assistance) into Latin America during the 1980s as financial aid or debt relief, it would be a mistake to ignore or underestimate the importance of the commodity trade between Japan and Latin America. In particular, the constant and stable import of raw materials and other natural resources from Latin America is vital to a Japan that is "highly industrialized," yet lacking in its natural resources (see Table 3). For example, the Japanese steel industry produces approximately 100 million tons of crude steel per year, but imports almost 100 percent of its iron ore. More than 20 million tons of iron ore (representing more than a fifth of Japan's total annual iron ore imports) come from one Latin American producer: Brazil.

Second, over the last decade, there was a slowdown in Japanese direct investments to Latin America seeking a return on that investment. The bulk of investment went to securing iron ore, lumber, and other natural resources on a long-term basis for Japanese industries.

Third, I would like to make a few comments on a US-Japanese partnership or cooperative scenario for Latin America. In general, I agree with Stallings's comments that both the content and framework of cooperation between the two countries are still unclear. I know from my own experiences, however, that there are numerous success stories in the US and Japanese private sectors, where the import and export trade between the United States and Latin America gradually increased through the strenuous efforts of Japanese traders. In this sense, underlying US-Japanese cooperation already exists, though it is not apparent at first glance. From the Japanese perspective, it makes more sense to consider our relationship with Latin America within the context of a

## Table 3.   Japanese Trade with Latin America

(millions of dollars)

| | Total Trade | | Trade with Latin America | | | |
|------|---------|---------|---------|-------|---------|-------|
| | *Exports* | *Imports* | *Exports* | *(%)* | *Imports* | *(%)* |
| 1973 | 36,930 | 38,314 | 2,761 | 7.5 | 1,955 | 5.1 |
| 1974 | 55,536 | 62,111 | 5,065 | 9.1 | 2,713 | 4.4 |
| 1975 | 55,758 | 57,863 | 4,765 | 8.5 | 2,524 | 4.4 |
| 1976 | 67,255 | 64,799 | 5,013 | 7.5 | 2,465 | 3.8 |
| 1977 | 80,495 | 70,809 | 6,292 | 7.8 | 3,065 | 4.3 |
| 1978 | 97,543 | 79,343 | 6,621 | 6.8 | 3,047 | 3.8 |
| 1979 | 103,032 | 110,672 | 6,555 | 6.4 | 4,517 | 4.1 |
| 1980 | 129,807 | 140,528 | 8,917 | 6.9 | 5,700 | 4.1 |
| 1981 | 152,030 | 143,290 | 10,516 | 6.9 | 6,669 | 4.7 |
| 1982 | 138,831 | 131,931 | 9,086 | 6.5 | 6,268 | 4.8 |
| 1983 | 146,927 | 126,393 | 6,391 | 4.3 | 6,462 | 5.1 |
| 1984 | 170,114 | 136,503 | 8,549 | 5.0 | 7,230 | 5.3 |
| 1985 | 175,638 | 129,539 | 8,486 | 4.8 | 6,242 | 4.8 |
| 1986 | 209,151 | 126,408 | 9,494 | 4.5 | 6,194 | 4.9 |
| 1987 | 229,221 | 149,515 | 8,760 | 3.8 | 6,355 | 4.3 |
| 1988 | 264,917 | 187,354 | 9,297 | 3.5 | 8,313 | 4.4 |

Source: Latin American Association, Tokyo, Japan.

tripartite partnership consisting of the European Community (EC), the United States, and Japan for a number of reasons:

• Because of its historical, cultural, and ethnic links, the Japanese people perceive Latin America as having an inherent European orientation.
• Japan ranks as the third largest trade partner for Latin America following the United States and the EC.
• The cooperation of EC countries in forging debt relief for Latin America seems indispensable to the reactivation of the Latin American economy.

Fourth, a brief analysis of Latin America's lack of success in exporting its industrial goods to the Japanese market is in order. According to statistics published by JETRO (Japan External Trade Organization), the total amount of Japanese imports from abroad in 1989 was $210 billion. Out of that figure, 50 percent was manufactured goods. This 50 percent ratio of imported manufactured goods in Japan is obviously low compared with the United States (which is above 80 percent) and the EC (which is slightly below 80 percent). Further, the total import of manufactured goods in Japan in 1988 breaks down as follows: the United States, 26% ($26 billion); the EC, 23% ($20 billion); Southeast Asia, 25% (25 billion); China, 5% ($4.6 billion); and the Middle East, 2% ($1.6 billion). These figures clearly imply that there is a slim chance for Latin America, at least at the moment, to break in and increase its market share of manufactured goods in Japan. I do not believe that Latin American manufactured goods are encountering unfair treatment in the Japanese market when compared with other foreign competitors.

## Latin America's Disadvantages

Currently, Latin America has some inherent disadvantages because of the following factors: price competitiveness, technology and quality of the product, punctuality and stability of the delivery of the products and aftercare service, and matching with the taste and requirements of the consumers in Japan. Of these, the principal factor is price competitiveness. Even if the FOB price (at loading port) is competitive, Latin American countries are often handicapped by distance. For example, the sea route between Rio de Janeiro and Tokyo is about 12,000 nautical miles. The distance between Rio de Janeiro and Philadelphia is only 4,500 nautical miles. If basic conditions such as loading, unloading terms, and size of vessel are the same compared to world competitors, the longer distance naturally results in a higher freight rate. In the case of Latin American natural resource exports to Japan, extraordinary efforts have been made to minimize the expense of shipping and to remain competitive upon arrival in Japan. In general, the reduction of the ocean freight cost is one of the key elements for survival in trade.

Fifth, I would like to make a few comments on the role and contribution of Japanese companies engaged in trade and investment with Latin America. Stallings's analysis of the role and function of Japanese trading companies seems to be helpful as a guide to foreigners in understanding the special features of Japanese trading companies. Some of her figures, however, should be analyzed further.

Undoubtedly, globalization and localization of business operation seems to be an emerging trend everywhere, including in Latin America. The diversification of trade by Japanese traders in Latin America seeking to expand "inter-third trade" (between Latin America and the United States, Asia, Europe, etc.) seems to be a new direction—a bold challenge for the 1990s. Incidentally, Japanese exports to Latin America are likely to remain sluggish in the 1990s.

In closing, several comments are in order on the future role of Japan in Latin America. First, Japan should intensify its efforts to use more official development assistance funds and human resources to assist democratization and reform in Latin America. As a starting point, free presidential elections, held in close cooperation with the United States, Europe, the Organization of American States, and the United Nations, should be encouraged.

Second, Japan can strengthen its cooperation with Latin America through the exchange of qualified human resources for the purposes of improving productivity, quality control, managerial skills, industrial training, and the transfer of technology. Third, in order for Latin American countries to restore their economies, they need the full support and cooperation of the creditor nations—the United States, Japan, and the EC—on a long-term basis to reduce their debt burden. Last, but certainly not least, it is extremely important to unite our forces to assist Latin America in stimulating economic growth by increasing exports to the world market. Unlike simple financing, the export trade can provide broader opportunities in employment, training, and transfer of technology, and its development should have a favorable impact on the growth of domestic production as well.

As the saying goes, "Donde hay ganas, hay camino," or in other words: "Where there is a will, there is a way." The outlook of Latin America's economy is bleak and uncertain, but with the newfound resolve of its people for peace and development, we can hope for its revival.

# 4

# The Uruguay Round of Multilateral Trade Negotiations: Implications for Latin America

## Luis Abugattas

This chapter addresses two basic issues. The first section analyzes the development of the Uruguay Round of the General Agreement on Tariffs and Trade (GATT) during the past four years. Its emphasis is on the difficulties confronted during the negotiating process and to those elements that will allow the trade round to conclude with positive and balanced results that are acceptable to all participants. The second section of the chapter analyzes the state of the negotiations in core areas of the Uruguay Round, and focuses on Latin America's interests and positions on those issues.

The outcome of the Uruguay Round negotiations are of great importance to the development prospects of Latin America and for future hemispheric relations. Since the second half of the 1980s, most Latin American countries have progressively implemented structural adjustment programs that substantially modify past development policies. The countries of the region have come to realize that maintaining high protection levels for domestic markets, along with the burgeoning growth of the state bureaucracy and its meddling in markets have led to serious distortions in relative prices. Not surprisingly, these factors make it impossible for national production to compete internationally.

Countries in the region are trying to correct the prevailing situation by making structural changes that rationalize foreign trade policies, drastically reduce tariff levels, properly manage the exchange rate, and accelerate the privatization and modernization of productive structures through the sound operation of market forces. In short, a liberal revolution is sweeping through the region. The prospects for the current efforts of Latin American nations depend on a stable and predictable international trade environment that guarantees adequate access to foreign markets and abolishes the restrictions imposed on Latin American exports—actual or potential—by the major trading partners. The Uruguay Round must guarantee this kind of access. It would be ironic if, now that the region has opted for a liberal path to development, the industrialized nations backed away from their commitment to a liberal world order.

Furthermore, those Latin American governments that are implementing the structural adjustment programs face strong domestic opposition from industrialists, labor, and other affected interest groups. In fact, a number of recently elected administrations either came to power because of their opposition to drastic adjustment measures, or ignored such measures entirely in their electoral platforms. To a large extent, the permanence of liberal programs depends on clear signals from the international community in favor of a liberal trade regime. Otherwise, it will be extremely difficult to build and consolidate the required legitimacy for those programs or a social support base for liberalization efforts. Failure of the Uruguay Round will weaken the domestic position of those groups that are promoting liberal reforms in Latin America, and could open the way for a drastic reversal of existing liberal reforms in the near future.

Latin America has enthusiastically embraced President George Bush's Enterprise for the Americas Initiative (EAI), which calls for a hemispheric-wide free trade zone.[1] A number of countries have already signed bilateral agreements with the United States creating commissions on trade and investment as a forum to discuss such issues. Furthermore, Latin American integration groupings, such as the Andean Pact and the Southern Cone Common Market, have stated their willingness to subscribe to trade and investment agreements with the United States.

The agendas of the EAI and Uruguay Round address overlapping considerations. A balanced result in the multilateral trade negotiations, setting clear norms and disciplines, would certainly facilitate the establishment of free trade between the United States and Latin American countries or groupings. It is important that the resulting agreements take into account the preoccupations and interests of all affected parties; if they do not, complications will arise as each issue will have to be negotiated on a country-by-country basis. Thus, any bilateral or regional agreement must be compatible with the rights and obligations conferred to the parties by the multilateral agreements generated by the Uruguay Round.

The Uruguay Round constitutes the principal forum for negotiating conditions for market access. Its results will establish the general framework within which Latin America could negotiate future trade agreements with the United States. This is of special relevance for the most volatile issues in trade relations between the region and the United States, such as textiles and the apparel trade, agricultural and tropical products, and non-tariff barriers, among others.

## The Uruguay Round: Current Status

Trade ministers from more than ninety-two countries met at the Uruguayan resort of Punta del Este in September 1986 to launch a new round of global trade discussions. Initially proposed by the United States, and later supported by other industrial nations, the agreement to inaugurate a new round of negotiations took a full week to craft. Through their trade ministers and representatives, GATT contracting parties drafted the Declaration of Punta del Este, thus beginning only the eighth round of GATT negotiations since the agreement was first promulgated in 1948.

The Uruguay Round has four objectives:

- To open international trade by reducing tariff and non-tariff barriers.
- To strengthen the institutional capacity of GATT itself.
- To expand the range of GATT coverage to include new areas such as textiles and agriculture.
- To extend the scope of GATT into newly emerging issues of international trade, such as services, trade-related aspects of intellectual property rights (TRIP's), and trade-related investment measures (TRIM's).

Fifteen negotiating groups were established to cover these issues. With a daunting array of difficult issues to address, the Uruguay Round is regarded as one of the most ambitious series of global trade negotiations since the end of World War II. As one observer has stated, "in the history of international co-operation there has almost certainly never been a negotiation as complicated as the Uruguay Round."[2]

According to the time frame agreed on at the Uruguay Round, the Trade Negotiations Committee (TNC) convened at the ministerial level in Brussels on December 3, 1990, to conclude the trade round. Instead, the ministerial meeting collapsed and the negotiating process broke up. The contracting parties agreed to prolong the negotiations and the participating trade ministers adjourned their four-year effort to reform the trading system. Although the ministers did adopt a final declaration, they failed to sign any final agreements.

The collapse of the Brussels negotiations is generally attributed to an impasse on agricultural considerations.[3] A review of the "Draft Final Act," however, reveals the lack of agreement in most of the major areas of negotiation.[4] Strong antagonisms and profound differences remain with respect to, among others, textiles, services, TRIP's, TRIM's, subsidies and countervailing measures, safeguards, dumping, and balance of payment restrictions (Art. XVIII.b). Even market access negotiations have not produced significant results. Nevertheless, some progress was made in clarifying certain articles of GATT and some of the agreements and arrangements of the Multilateral Trade Negotiations (MTN's).

The current state of the negotiations is one of uncertainty. Although the Brussels meeting was a complete failure, the ministers made an effort to keep the Uruguay Round alive, allowing for a "cooling off" period. They agreed that the negotiations should move back to Geneva, and they instructed the director general of GATT to determine possible avenues of consensus so that negotiations could resume. They also agreed that future negotiations would be based on the "Draft Final Act." Thus, participants may not be compromised by any agreements or offers made during the TNC meeting in Brussels.

Progress has been made since the Brussels meeting. At the request of Minister Hector Gros Spiel, chairman of the TNC at the ministerial level, GATT's director general Arthur Dunkel conducted consultations with the major trading partners in an effort to resolve differences in all major areas of disagreement. Furthermore, at the director general's insistence, an informal meeting of the TNC was convened on January 15, 1991, to keep the Third World delegates informed and to provide transparency to the consultations.

The first two months of 1991 were intense. The director general established a process involving bilateral and plurilateral consultations. This process, which has been described as "consultations in concentric circles,"[5] was aimed at producing a "platform" for future negotiations in agriculture and use it to resume negotiations in all areas of the Uruguay Round.

During this period, bilateral negotiations were held between the United States and the European Community (EC). Discussions over agriculture with members of the Cairns Group also took place. The EC met January 28-29, 1991, with senior officials from six Latin American countries (Argentina, Brazil, Colombia, Chile, Mexico and Uruguay—all members of the Cairns Group with the exception of Mexico). At the meeting, the EC emphasized the importance of a multilateral trading system and suggested that the six countries curtail some of their more ambitious desires in an effort to save the negotiations.

Not withstanding the efforts made by all of the parties, it proved impossible to produce a basic platform on agriculture that would serve as a launching point for serious negotiations on the issue, and allow the overall process of the Uruguay Round a fresh start. This failure made it clear that the negotiations would not be concluded by the beginning of 1991. The focus then shifted to avoiding the final collapse of the Round by restarting the negotiating process. For this purpose, principal participants in the negotiations were called together for meetings between February 20 and 25, 1991, to discuss the possibility of resuming the Round. Only those delegations that had contributed in particular areas were invited to participate at the meetings.

At the meetings, the director general presented his assessment of the different negotiating groups' situations based on his consultations. No country was permitted to make a presentation or debate any issue. Finally, the TNC met on February 26. There, the director general stated: "my consultations have led me to conclude that I now have all the elements necessary for us to put the negotiations back on track," and proposed a work agenda. The committee concurred with the assessment and officially resumed the negotiations, but it failed to establish any chronological framework for the Round.

Even though the negotiating process has officially resumed, the future prospects of the Uruguay Round remain unclear. Participants have expressed a "cautious optimism" about the possible results of the negotiations, but consultations carried out by the director general have not produced any significant break in the entrenched issues that faced the ministers at Brussels. In fact, crucial negotiating groups have not moved forward much since the midterm review of December 1988.[6]

The prospects for success in the Uruguay Round are very fragile. In an attempt to achieve consensus on crucial issues, negotiations are continuing on a technical level. Yet, the real prospects for success rest on important political decisions that have to be made by the major trading partners.

The short-term prospects for success of the Round depend on two fundamental factors. First, the EC must clearly signal its decision to seriously negotiate the liberalization of international agricultural trade. Without this, it will be nearly impossible to maintain, let alone accelerate, the pace of the overall negotiating process and guarantee a real compromise on other issues. Up to now, the EC has transmitted very ambiguous signals. Second, the US Congress must extend the "fast-track" authority of the US executive so that he may be able to negotiate more freely. In the absence of a clear mandate, participants will not take negotiations seriously. In fact, it is unlikely that the participants will engage in any substantive negotiations until a mandate is provided.

## Obstacles to a Successful Completion of the Uruguay Round

In terms of its objectives, its dynamics, and the international environment in which it is taking place, the Uruguay Round is substantially different from previous trade rounds. Technological innovations in the productive processes and international transactions, the inadequacy of existing—and woefully outdated—legal and institutional arrangements, and the change in the relative positioning of major trading partners to international labor have inspired novel initiatives in the context of managing the new international economics.[7]

The Uruguay Round represents a unique rule-making exercise; it embraces problems and solutions far more complicated than those ever contemplated in earlier GATT negotiations. It thus demands a profound revision of basic trade concepts and definitions. Furthermore, many of the Round's proposals infringe upon national sovereignty substantially more than those discussed in previous rounds. This, added to GATT's institutional capabilities and improvements in the mechanisms and instruments used to enforce multilateral norms and disciplines, has introduced a high degree of complexity to the negotiations. As a result, the evolution of the Uruguay Round has been plagued with difficulties. For the first time in the history of GATT, the ministers met at Punta del Este without the consensus required to launch the trade round. The negotiations were initiated only after the ministers reached a last-minute agreement for the liberalization of services and trade. The ministerial meeting, held in Montreal, December 5-9, 1988, for the midterm review of the negotiations had to be suspended. Only in the April meeting of the TNC (Geneva, April 5-12, 1989) could a very loose final declaration be adopted.

The TNC meeting of July 23-28, 1990, was expected to generate basic agreements in the different negotiating groups and provide the impetus for final negotiations in Brussels. The result of the meeting, however, disappointed everyone. Likewise, the meeting scheduled for November 12, 1990, to evaluate the negotiations according to the provisions of Section G of the Punta del Este Declaration, had to be cancelled. Brazilian ambassador Rubens Ricuepero explained, "in the current state of affairs it is clearly impossible to carry out a detailed assessment of the progress in relation to special and differential treatment for developing countries in the negotiations."[8]

In mid-November the director general of GATT stated that "some major political decisions are urgent and essential and it is not an exaggeration to say that the Brussels meeting is now in jeopardy."[9] The director general was advised to delay the TNC meeting at the ministerial level until there was some basis of agreement in the more hotly debated issues. Nevertheless, the decision was taken to carry on with the ill-fated December 1990 meeting.

Beyond the complexity of the negotiating agenda, the delicate connections between the different issues, and the short period of time allowed for the process, other elements have considerably added to the difficulties that negotiators have faced since 1986. These difficulties have to be confronted in the post-Brussels stage.

Still, the Punta del Este Declaration is a carefully drafted document that expresses the delicate balance of interests achieved among the contracting parties. Indeed, it made it possible for the trade round to be launched. Nevertheless, during the course of the negotiations, proposals have complicated the negotiating process and affected the development of the Uruguay Round in a number of ways:

- In some negotiating groups, in particular with respect to TRIP's and TRIM's, the objective of the negotiating mandate has changed. Latin American countries have led a strong reaction by developing countries to produce a deadlock in the process.
- Throughout the negotiations, developed countries have tried to curtail the special and differential treatment generally given to developing nations under GATT (Part IV). Although the Punta del Este Declaration clearly states that the developed countries should not expect the developing countries to make contributions that are incon-

sistent with their own development and financial and trade needs, they have demanded reciprocity of negotiated commitments. These demands are of particular concern in such areas as textiles, tropical products, and services.

- Although the Punta del Este Declaration mandates the development of balanced agreements, current negotiations are asymmetric. Developed countries demand strong multilateral commitments with regard to services, intellectual property, TRIM's, and TRIP's. Meanwhile, they have been unwilling to compromise on issues of primary importance to developing countries (e.g., agriculture, textiles, natural resource-based products, market access negotiations). Thus, it is unlikely that the developing countries will be flexible in meeting the developed countries' demands. Furthermore, given that contracting parties agreed in Punta del Este to treat the various negotiations as a single undertaking, the possible imbalance in current negotiations could make it difficult to embrace any resulting agreements.

Latin American and Caribbean countries formulated a joint declaration in July 1990, which emanated from the Fifth Coordination Meeting of the Economic System of Latin America. They stated, inter alia, that "the results of the negotiations in the Uruguay Round will be acceptable for the Latin American and Caribbean countries only if they respond to the specific mandates of the Punta del Este Declaration," and that "the region will resist any attempt to redefine or to extend the principles agreed for the conduct of the negotiations."[10] The majority of developing countries support this position and demand that the Punta del Este Declaration be adhered to in the negotiating process. The prospects to unlock the negotiations in core issues depends on this condition.

The evolution of the negotiations reflect the difficulties in reconciling the existing trade regime with the new world realities. The difficulties encountered during the Uruguay Round have been particularly exacerbated by the absence of hegemonic leadership. In contrast to the earlier post-World War II period in which progressive liberalization of world trade and the establishment and maintenance of an international trade regime were possible under US leadership, no country currently has the capability to impose its will and conclude the negotiations.

The Uruguay Round thus imposes a great challenge to the world community: to create a pattern of order for international economic transactions by means of a meaningful cooperative effort. This will require significant changes in the attitudes and behavior of the major participants in the next stage of the process. Furthermore, it also becomes evident that no successful results can be expected in the Uruguay Round without full participation of the developing countries. Developing countries can no longer be ignored in any global cooperative effort. The new role of these countries was already evident at the Montreal meeting, where the Latin American nations were able to disrupt the conference when it became apparent that the United States and Europe could not reach an agreement on agriculture. Although there had been progress in every other negotiating area, Latin America insisted that without an agreement on agriculture, no other agreements could be ratified.

In the same vein, the developing countries participated decisively at Brussels. With their firm decision to resist any attempt to impose a ready-made package put together by a few participants and presented at the last minute on a "take it or leave it basis," there was obviously an attitude at work that significantly contributed to the final collapse of the ministerial meeting.

The third element that conspired against a smooth development of the negotiations and contributed to hardening the positions of many participants was the way in which the negotiations were conducted. The major trading partners attempted to resolve their outstanding issues through private consultations in "green room" meetings. Most participants were thus excluded from the deliberations and then later presented with draft documents that supposedly represented the consensus of the negotiators.

The issue of lack of transparency in the process erupted during the midterm review meeting during which the president of the TNC was strongly criticized by developing countries. For example, the Chilean delegate stated, "in no other international forum is there so much talk about transparency, and in no other one we have witnessed a less transparent process in decision making. This fact is one of the principal reasons that makes it difficult to reach agreements." The problem was further aggravated during the last stages of the negotiations. In a joint statement issued at the Brussels meeting, the developing countries pointed out that "their preoccupation with the lack of transparency of the negotiations was due, among other factors, to the attempt to solve outstanding issues through bilateral consultations among the major trading partners." A necessary condition for the negotiations to advance in early 1991 is that a comprehensive reformulation of the negotiating methods be undertaken. Full and adequate participation must be guaranteed to all participants and decisionmaking should be based on generalized consensus as is the norm in GATT.

Finally, an evaluation of the Uruguay Round must take into account the profound changes and the speed of transformation that the international system has experienced since the Round was launched. Since 1986, key events have had an impact on the positions and priorities of the major participants:

- The end of the Cold War and reforms in Eastern Europe and the Soviet Union that have created new challenges and opportunities for the industrialized nations, especially the EC (these events also significantly reduced the leverage of the United States in its bilateral negotiations with EC countries).
- The German unification and the impact on the position of that country with respect to the agricultural negotiations.
- The economic recession that has revived protectionist sentiments in the major trading partners, and that cast doubts about the political commitment to accept any final agreement.
- The continuing and unresolved debt crisis, and the processes of economic stabilization and structural adjustment put in practice by developing countries.
- The Gulf Crisis that diverted the attention of the world's senior political leaders in the crucial stage of the multilateral trade negotiations.

## Developments and Prospects of the Negotiations

This section presents a brief assessment of the state of the negotiations in the crucial negotiating groups. Special attention is paid to the interests and the position of the Latin American countries. The discussion is organized under three major headings: market access, normative negotiations, and "new issues."

*Market Access.* The negotiations in the areas of tariffs and non-tariff measures, tropical products, agriculture, textiles, and natural resource-based products represent the priority areas for the Latin American countries, as well as for the rest of the developing countries. It is in these areas that the Uruguay Round can provide concrete benefits to the countries of the region. Unfortunately, the results in market access negotiations, at least so far, are not very promising.

*Tariff Negotiations.* The contracting parties agreed in Montreal that the tariff reductions should be, at the very least, equivalent to those agreed upon during the Tokyo Round, that is, at least a 30 percent reduction of the 1986 tariff levels. Even though there were proposals to apply a mathematical formula for tariff reductions, in practice the negotiating process became an offer/petition one. The United States never accepted the formula approach.

Most participants have presented an initial offer of tariff reduction, and have engaged in bilateral negotiations with their principal suppliers in an offer/petition process. At this stage, it is not possible to make an evaluation of the results for Latin America of these negotiations. Nevertheless, some estimates set the overall tariff reduction achieved through the initial offers at 15 percent of the 1986 levels, far below the goal set for the trade round.

The United States is the most important market for Latin American exporters. The United States imported $43 billion worth of goods in 1988; 74.4 percent of which were subjected to tariffs. Although the initial tariff cuts offered by the United States to the whole region hover around 27 percent of the weighted average—close to the goal set for the trade round—each reduction is subject to conditions by product and measure based on reciprocity of tariff cuts or elimination of non-tariff barriers.[11]

The Latin American countries are dissatisfied with the reductions offered by the principal developed countries. Some of the offers, such as those related to agricultural products, are conditional. Others are of limited scope and do not address the problems of tariff progression and tariff peaks. These problems must be considered for negotiations to progress.

Most Latin American countries have made important tariff reduction offers and have even offered to bind their tariff schedules. Furthermore, a number of countries in the region have drastically reduced their tariff levels and eliminated all non-tariff trade barriers. Notwithstanding the Montreal agreement to recognize and give due credit to such actions, the major trading partners have shown little acknowledgement and appreciation for these efforts.

*Tropical Products.*[12] Tropical products represent only 3 percent of world trade, but are significant in economic terms for most of Latin America. Trade liberalization in this area has been considered a priority in the Uruguay Round, and market access offers were negotiated as early as the Montreal meeting.

The offers tabled as of July 1990 by the industrialized countries would have created an additional trade in tropical products of about $746 million, that is, a 3 percent increase of the value of imports in 1986. Interestingly, the principal beneficiaries of the increased trade would be developed countries that would see their exports of processed tropical products to other developed countries increase by $457 million. For developing countries, the offers only imply an increase of 1.7 percent of their exports of tropical products or a net gain of $250 million, 95 percent of which is explained by increased market access to the EC. Nevertheless, as coffee accounts for 75 percent of trade covered by the offers, the gains of trade liberalization would not even compensate for losses generated by the collapse of the International Coffee Agreement.

*Agriculture.* Agricultural trade liberalization has become the most intractable issue in the Uruguay Round. Negotiations are aimed at achieving greater liberalization of trade in agriculture and bringing all measures that affect import access and export competition under strengthened and more operationally effective GATT rules and disciplines. The main problem surrounding agricultural trade is the cost of agricultural policies in the countries of the Organisation for Economic Cooperation and Development—estimated at around $250 billion a year—and the distortions that such policies cause in international trade.

The overall negotiation process has focused on reducing border restrictions, internal support measures, export subsidies, and sanitary and phytosanitary barriers and measures. It is estimated that the liberalization of agricultural trade could result in an additional $50 billion of export income to the most efficient agricultural producer nations during the next decade. Unfortunately, negotiations on this issue have been at an impasse since the midterm review. Now, because of the antagonism created, the future of the Uruguay Round rests on the outcome of a showdown between the United States and the Cairns Group on one hand, and the EC on the other.

The United States and the Cairns Group have made separate offers for agricultural trade reform. They call for a 75 percent reduction of internal support measures, tariffication of all existing border measures and their reduction by 75 percent, and a reduction of all export subsidies by 90 percent, all to be completed within ten years.

For its part, and after much deliberation, the EC offered to reduce the aggregate measures of support to its agricultural sector by 30 percent in ten years. The EC also introduced the concept of rebalancing, by which the liberalization in some areas would be compensated by the development of restrictive measures affecting other products. The measure is to be based on 1986 levels, so the actual offer constitutes only a 15 percent reduction of support beyond what has already been implemented.

During the Brussels meeting, the EC, followed by Japan and Korea, rejected a compromise solution presented by the president of the negotiating group. The solution called for a 30 percent reduction from the 1990 levels in the three areas of negotiation (internal support, tariffication, and reduction) during a ten-year period and discarded the rebalancing concept.

The liberalization of agricultural trade is of the foremost importance to Latin American countries. Accordingly, Argentina, Brazil, Chile, Colombia, and Uruguay have participated actively in the Cairns Group, as they depend heavily on agricultural exports. In a joint communication, the countries stated that "for the success of the Uruguay Round and the consequent acceptance of a final package, it is a prerequisite that adequate results are achieved that will lead to a substantial liberalization of trade."[13] Furthermore, Latin America has demanded special and differential treatment for developing countries during the transition period, thus allowing them greater flexibility in applying their domestic agricultural policies.

Some countries, Peru and Jamaica in particular, have been active in the ranks of net food importers. It is estimated that the liberalization of agricultural trade will raise the international prices of basic food staples between 10 and 30 percent depending on the product. The food importing countries demand that the final agreement consider the negative impact of world agricultural reform on their economies. They demand that corrective measures be undertaken during the transition period in the form of financial assistance, concessional sales, food aid, and agricultural development programs.

Efforts made after the Brussels meeting by the director general to reach a basic platform on agriculture did not produce tangible results. The EC has reaffirmed its position, demanding that other participants lower their expectations about what can be achieved with regard to agricultural trade liberalization. At the February 20, 1991, meeting, Director General Dunkel said that "my consultations confirm that participants agree to conduct negotiations to achieve specific binding commitments on each of the following areas: domestic support, market access, export competition; and to reach an agreement on sanitary and phytosanitary issues." He called for technical work to begin immediately to facilitate these negotiations. As no country refuted the statement, its approval could mean a minor advance in the negotiations, providing the EC agrees to compromise in the different areas covered by the negotiations.

*Textiles.* The Declaration of Punta del Este provides that "negotiations in the area of textiles and clothing shall aim to formulate modalities that would permit the eventual integration of this sector into the GATT on the basis of strengthened GATT rules and disciplines, thereby also contributing to the objective of further liberalization of trade." The agreement's aim is to dismantle the Multifiber Agreement (MFA), which has subjected imports of textiles and clothing from developing countries to bilaterally negotiated quotas for nearly thirty years.

Textiles and clothing trade is estimated at $180 billion a year. Due to the export potential of the Latin American countries, and the difficulties they have encountered in gaining access to the markets of developed countries, this trade is of great importance for the region.

Because textile and clothing trade is a sensitive issue for developed countries, the negotiators are far from producing a comprehensive agreement. Although the industrialized nations have imposed a special regime for textile trade on developing countries based on the time required by the developing nations to restructure their domestic industries, they are demanding a further period of transition (from ten to fifteen years) before the sector is finally integrated into GATT.

Integration into GATT would be achieved in three stages. A given percentage would be integrated in each stage. Some proposals call for 10 percent to be integrated initially, then 10 percent, 25 percent in the first and second stages, and 55 percent at the end of the transition period. Furthermore, developed countries demand strong liberalizing commitments and other conditions from developing countries as a requirement to dismantle the MFA. The Latin American countries maintain that this position is unacceptable because no concessions can be demanded that put an end to a system that is a derogation of GATT.

For their part, the Latin American countries demand special treatment for developing countries that are small exporters. This treatment must account for base levels of exports and differing growth rates. The Latin American countries further demand that the developed countries agree to reduce their own tariff levels. In this matter, the US offer has been minimal, a 7 percent reduction of a high average tariff of 18.4 percent.

*Natural Resource-Based Products.* World trade in natural resource-based products is about $140 billion. Cited by the developing countries as a key area of concern, a separate negotiating group was established. The group's objective is to eliminate trade barriers and create a more predictable market.

Initially, negotiations were to cover nonferrous metals, forestry, and fisheries, focusing on the elimination of tariff and non-tariff barriers as well as problems of tariff escalation. The industrialized countries demanded to expand negotiations to include energy products, domestic policy, access to resources, among others. The United States, for example, demanded to negotiate such broad issues as dual pricing of natural resources, related export restrictions, local processing requirements, subsidies, and certain government ownership practices. As a result of the over expansion of issues, the negotiations collapsed and the issues subsumed by the negotiating group on tariffs and non-tariff barriers.

*Normative Areas.* With respect to negotiations in the normative areas, there remains a number of issues that have to be resolved for the Uruguay Round to produce adequate and balanced results. Two issues are of crucial importance for Latin America. First, the issue of dumping, subsidies, and countervailing measures must be considered. Second, the debt problems of developing countries must be addressed.

With respect to dumping, subsidies, and countervailing measures, no agreement in the negotiations has yet been crafted and no comprehensive draft text was provided for the Brussels meeting. Strong differences persist between the participants. Some countries demand that the practices and instruments of some of the major trading partners be multilateralized. Other participants focus on antidumping measures. These countries call for the development of investigatory mechanisms and strict enforcement of the rules.

Dumping, subsidies, and countervailing measures are of particular interest to the Latin American countries because of the proliferation of these measures and their potential abuse; they are well aware that the measures can be used to restrict legitimate trade flows, thus amounting to a "new type protectionism."

Also of importance to Latin America is the attempt by the developed countries to start negotiations aimed at limiting their rights under Article XVIII:B to the adoption of corrective measures when confronting balance of payments difficulties. In this respect, the Latin American countries maintain that they will not permit the balance of rights and obligations under the provision to be modified.

*"New Issues."* The agenda of the Uruguay Round includes three new controversial issues: TRIP's, TRIM's, and services. Even if these issues are handled in separate negotiating groups, they are closely linked as integral parts of a single global issue: the redefinition of the domain of the nation state at the world level and the creation and protection of competitive advantages. The developed countries seek the establishment of a multilateral framework that would include all aspects of transnational activities and all relevant international transactions. It is in these issues that the confrontation along North-South lines is clearly evident.

*Trade-Related Intellectual Property Rights (TRIP's).* Because technological innovations may provide their countries of origin with comparative trade advantages, the economic management of ideas, data information, and overall know-how has become a strategic business and national concern. The generation, access, and protection of knowledge have emerged as concerns crucial to all nations.

The proposals put forth by the industrial nations aim to change and reinforce the systems of intellectual property rights protection in some fundamental ways. First, they would replace the current system based on national jurisdiction and loose international conventions, like the Berne Convention and the Universal Copyright Convention, for an effective multilateral agreement with wide participation. Proposals include (a) the creation of border controls with effective penalties against transgressions, (b) the development of national standards that safeguard property rights, (c) measures that ensure that intellectual property rights measures will not act as obstacles to trade, and (d) the extension of international dispute settlement procedures to provide effective sanctions. A second component is the extension of the coverage on intellectual property rights protection to new areas not adequately addressed by most national systems. This is an area of major concern for the technological leaders. Current regulations for the most part have been surpassed by rapid technological innovation, and software, semiconductors, biotechnology, and other innovations are not effectively protected at the world level. A third component is the extension of the duration of protection. A fourth component calls for the effective domestic enforcement of intellectual property rights.

The inclusion of TRIP's in GATT would have serious implications for the developing countries. Until now each country has established in accordance with its interests the degree of protection it allowed to technological innovations. The establishment of an international system for intellectual property rights protection will force developing countries to follow international norms whose objectives may not coincide with their national interests.

The introduction of a new international system and the execution of those rights by the technological leaders would mean the dismantling of those national regulations designed to promote and protect domestic industry with infant technological capabilities. As a result, endogenous technological development will be difficult for developing countries. They will be reduced to a growing technological dependence on the industrial world. Furthermore, the cost of acquiring new technology in a monopolistic price setting, some of which has the character of a public good, would imply a significant cost in terms of foreign currency to the developing countries, widening the structural imbalances in their foreign accounts. The US International Trade Commission estimates that US industry alone would receive between $43-102 billion of the income if intellectual property rights are adequately enforced.

Although a draft text for the TRIP's negotiations was produced for the Brussels meeting, no agreement has been reached on any of the substantive issues. There are several outstanding issues. First, there is much concern over "Gattability"; copyrights decisions covering computer programs must be reached. Second, patent law presents many important challenges. Patentable subject matter and exclusion, the term of protection, nonvoluntary licensing, and government use all await further clarifications. Third, issues revolving around procedural and enforcement mechanisms must be examined. Fourth, there is strong resistance to the protection of undisclosed information and to the extension of the protection for layout-designs of integrated circuits. In fact, negotiations on TRIP's have not progressed since 1987.

Regardless of what agreements are finally reached, developing countries will demand an adequate transition period. They maintain that such a period is necessary to allow them to restructure their productive capabilities. Some countries have linked this transition period with those agreed on for agriculture and textiles.

*Trade-Related Investment Measures (TRIM's).* Developed countries would like to create the basis for an international investment regime.

Until now the relationship between host country, foreign investors, and technology suppliers has been based on domestic legislation or, in some cases, on bilateral negotiations with the transnational corporations. In this context, it has been in the domain of the host state to determine the conditions under which it is willing to accept the presence of foreign direct investment in the country, and to set the requirements that the transnational corporations have had to fulfill in order to effectively contribute to the development objectives.

What the industrial countries are trying to implement through the GATT is an agreement that would eliminate the right of the host country to determine those issues, and instead subject those considerations to the general agreement. Industrial countries argue that Third World restrictions on local content, production, sales, exports, equity, and licensing requirements, as well as exchange and remittance restriction, distort trade and, as such, should be banned by GATT.

Negotiations in Geneva on TRIM's failed to yield an agreement or even a draft text for the Brussels meeting. The developed countries, in particular the United States and Japan, demand the enactment of general restriction prohibitions. Latin American countries maintain that sanctions must be doled out on a case-by-case basis. They argue that the objective of the negotiations is to correct trade distortions produced by restrictive investment measures and that each situation must be individually examined within this context. They therefore maintain that GATT regulations are sufficient.

*Services.* Contrary to all expectations, much progress has been made in the effort to liberalize the $600 billion a year service trade. In fact, the negotiators presented a draft agreement for services trade that could be accepted by most participants.

Agreement is possible because two important issues have substantially been resolved. Initially, and in a reversal of policy, the United States suggested that it would only confer Most Favored Nation (MFN) on a conditional country-by-country basis. Nevertheless, the United States later agreed to grant MFN status automatically in any service agreement provided that there was an accompanying package of specific market-opening agreements. Additionally, negotiators have produced major advances with regard to derogations; it was agreed that derogations would be minimal and subject to revision. It was also determined that civil aviation and maritime transport will be included in the initial derogations.

There are other issues pending, such as an agreement on financial services, and the extent of the commitments expected from developing countries, but these issues can be resolved with a minimum of political will.

## Prospects for the Negotiations

It is difficult to predict the outcome of future efforts and negotiations because of the very ambitious nature of the Uruguay Round and the rapidly changing international relations. At this moment, at least four possible scenarios can be visualized.

In the first scenario, the Uruguay Round is deemed an utter failure and the negotiating process is permanently tabled. Two circumstances could prompt this situation. The first possibility is that the EC refuses to seriously negotiate the liberalization of world agricultural trade. Latin American countries, among others, will not negotiate in the absence of clear and unambitious commitments for fundamental agricultural reforms. They do not want a repeat of the first four years of negotiating, culminating in a Brussels-style fiasco. Secondly, a US congressional refusal to extend the president's "fast-track" authority would cast serious doubts about the feasibility of enacting any final agreements and would reflect poorly upon the commitment of the United States.

The collapse of the negotiations would undermine the international trade regime and irretrievably weaken GATT. For Latin America, a collapse of the Uruguay Round would be a mixed blessing. Beyond agriculture, Latin America has little to gain from the Uruguay Round. Latin American agricultural exporters would suffer because they would lose the opportunity to access new markets, while importers would be forced to pay more for their food. A collapse of the multilateral trading system, however, would eliminate one of the few defense mechanisms that Latin American countries have in their bilateral trade relations with the United States.

A collapse of the Uruguay Round could lead to the establishment of regional trading blocs. Already, many observers argue that GATT is obsolete.[14] Latin American willingness to accept US terms for participation in the EAI would be enhanced under such a scenario. Despite the general enthusiasm for the new US initiative throughout Latin America, a rapid regional embrace of a new trading bloc would not be assured. After all, many Latin American countries have taken unilateral measures to restructure their economies and reduce trade barriers under the implicit assumption that such efforts would be rewarded by the developed countries.

A collapse of the Uruguay Round and hard-line conditions in the EAI negotiations, especially on TRIM's and TRIP's, would undermine the legitimacy of the region's political leaders who are pushing for closer trade relations. But as George Bush clearly indicated during his trip to South America in December 1990, hemispheric agreements could fill the void left by the collapse of the Uruguay Round. In fact, because of the difficulties outlined in the Uruguay Round, this second option may provide the best opportunity for Latin America.

A second possible scenario, if the Round encounters serious difficulties during the post-Brussels stage, is that of a "quick fix" on the basis of a minimum package that can be agreed upon by the major trading partners. This package would reflect the recognition that the objectives set for the Uruguay Round were too ambitious.[15] Under this scenario, the more confrontational issues would probably not be addressed; settlement would occur in at least six or seven areas in which there is currently some basis for consensus. Other issues would be left for a future round of multilateral trade negotiations.

Unfortunately, this quick fix could create a serious imbalance in the results for Latin America. While they probably would have to concede much ground on agricultural trade and other areas of interest for the region, the developed countries would still expect them to compromise on issues such as services and TRIP's.

In the third scenario, the Uruguay Round would be turned into a permanent process of trade negotiations in which the different trade issues would be settled without the benefit of any particular time schedules. This scenario is possible because of an agreement adopted in the TNC meeting of February 26, 1991. This option implies periodic decisionmaking with respect to those issues where consensus is reached. Nevertheless, this scenario has some important shortcomings. Firstly, it would make it impossible for any country to apply a cost-benefit framework in evaluating the final results of a series of agreements. This situation would certainly harden negotiating positions; each country would try to minimize the cost of its commitments on every issue. Secondly, it would mean an important departure from the Punta del Este Declaration, which stated that negotiations are to be considered a single undertaking. Thirdly, it would make it almost impossible to effectively evaluate the application of differential treatment for developing countries as mandated by the Declaration and demanded by developing countries.

In the fourth scenario, the US Congress would yield to the overwhelming popularity of President Bush and approve the extension of his "fast-track" authority. This scenario is highly probable because of the increasing possibilities that a free trade agreement will be signed with Mexico and because of the staggering political power wielded by a post-Persian Gulf War Bush. The likelihood of this extension could even be enhanced through concessions by the Bush administration; although US law provides for a two-year extension, the administration might suggest that it would use the procedures for a shorter period of time. This probable outcome, without any formal agreement by the TNC, in practice would set a clear time frame for the conclusion of the post-Brussels stage of the negotiations.

If the negotiations are to be successfully completed, countries must negotiate pragmatically, realistically, transparently, and in accordance with the clear mandates of the Punta del Este Declaration. Although it is impossible to accurately predict the actual outcome of the Uruguay Round, it is clear that negotiations must continue and agreements must be signed.

## NOTES

1. "Five Latin Ministers Embrace Free Trade," *The Wall Street Journal*, September 13, 1990.

2. *Financial Times*, December 8-9, 1990.

3. A *New York Times* editorial (December 8, 1990), "The Europeans Sabotage Trade," was especially harsh toward European resistance to modify farm policies.

4. "Draft Final Act Embodying the Results of the Uruguay Round of Multilateral Trade Negotiations" (MTN.TNC/W/35) of November 26, 1990.

5. *South-North Development Monitor*, no. 2537 (February 5, 1991).

6. The work program proposed by the director general for the second stage of the negotiations basically addresses the same issues that have

been unresolved since the Montreal meeting. See MTN.TNC/W/69 of February 26, 1991.

7. Luis Abugattas, "World Economic Restructuring and Multilateral Trade Negotiations: The New Issues in the Uruguay Round Problems and Prospects for Latin America" (Paper presented at the XIVth World Congress of the International Political Science Association, Washington, DC, August 28-September 1, 1988).

8. *Focus*, no. 76 (November 1990).

9. Ibid.

10. SELA, Declaración de los Países de América Latina y el Caribe sobre las Negociaciones de la Ronda Uruguay, July 17, 1990.

11. SELA, Evaluación sobre la Situación de la Ronda Uruguay de Negociaciones Comerciales Multilaterales Preparada por los Países de América Latina y el Caribe al 23 de Noviembre de 1990.

12. Data on this issue has been extracted from UNCTAD, "Uruguay Round Revised Offers of Tariffs Concession on Tropical Products (as of July 1990) the Potential Trade Impact," August 1990.

13. MTN/TNC/W/22.

14. See Gary Hufbauer, "Beyond GATT," *Foreign Policy*, no. 77 (Winter 1989-90): 64-76; and John H. Jackson, *Restructuring the GATT System* (New York: Council on Foreign Relations Press, 1990).

15. This kind of outcome was already suggested by the EC during the discussions previous to the restarting of the negotiations on February 26, 1991. See *South-North Development Monitor*, no. 2532 (January 29, 1991).

# US Policy, Latin America, and the Round

*Myles Frechette*

Luis Abugattas's chapter informs us about the General Agreement on Tariffs and Trade (GATT) system, which, to a large extent, operates by consensus. The US government would likely agree with Abugattas's conclusion: that the Uruguay Round is an ambitious undertaking. It would probably also second his claim that predicting the final outcome is, at this point in time, nearly impossible. Even US Trade Representative Carla Hills has said publicly that we have about a 20 percent chance of emerging from the Uruguay Round successfully. Other observers are more guarded in their opinion. The consensus-driven process of GATT, which tries to accommodate the views of numerous and disparate groups, however, makes it possible for Abugattas to present a version of events with which we simply do not agree. His interpretation of the Punta del Este agreement in Montreal is not our interpretation of what was agreed to there.

The value of Abugattas's chapter lies in how it details the Latin American view and sets that view apart from the vastly different outlook of the United States and the developing world. Our impression, however, is that the Latin American position is nowhere near as solid as Abugattas would suggest. When GATT was created in 1948, services, investment, intellectual property, and even agriculture were at the margins of a $60 billion a year world trading system. Today, it is estimated that world trade stands at $4 trillion annually and at least a third of that is not subject to any discipline. It is this neglected slice of the pie that we are trying to craft disciplines for in the current Uruguay Round. If we had tried to introduce disciplines into agricultural trade in 1948, there would have been many objections. Today, Latin Americans clearly see that it is important to discipline agriculture, particularly in curbing the

European Community's (EC) subsidies. Nevertheless, Latin America does not agree that services, investment, and intellectual property—which are a very large component of world trade today and a component that they also have a strong interest in—should be covered in the way that the United States and some of the other developing countries suggest.

The United States feels that it has been entirely consistent with the Punta del Este and Montreal mandates concerning the Round. Abugattas's chapter implies that the United States has gone astray, but we disagree. Abugattas states that the Uruguay Round has been a nontransparent process controlled by the developed countries. He quotes a Chilean representative who criticizes the president of the Trade Negotiations Committee for being nontransparent. That president, if I remember correctly, was Uruguayan. Contrary to Abugattas's assertion, this round has been one of the most transparent processes in the history of trade negotiation. Both in Montreal and in Brussels, Uruguay, Brazil, and Argentina played very active roles in the negotiations. As GATT is comprised of more than one hundred countries and organizations, it is obviously impossible, just on grounds of practicality, for everyone to be able to "shmooze" on a particular topic. Despite Abugattas's assertion, the developing countries are represented in the "green rooms" and I have talked personally with Latin American negotiators who were present at those discussions. The developing countries have been, and will continue to be, involved in negotiations to the extent that the Uruguay Round continues.

## Latin America's Benefits from the Round

Latin America has a great deal more to gain from the Round than progress in agricultural issues. Abugattas's position is disputed in public statements by a number of Latin American leaders who have openly supported positions that we also consider important. He also seems to suggest that Latin American interests have been somehow relegated to a sort of second-class status. This view is simply wrong. In agriculture, the Cairns Group came to us repeatedly, seeking reassurance that we would not sell out to the EC and abandon Latin America and other developing countries that export agricultural goods. This can hardly be presented as relegating the interests of the developing nations to second-class status.

Abugattas seems to embrace the notion that Latin Americans shouldn't be expected to take on significantly more responsibility in the world trading system. They should instead be extended special and differential treatment. Here again, honest people can differ about an interpretation, and we believe that the course of special and differential treatment being pushed by certain developing nations undermines global growth, development, and ultimately, the global trading system itself.

Abugattas exaggerates the extent of confrontation between Latin America and the United States. There are some very key differences, but they are overdrawn in his chapter. Abugattas also overstates the Latin American and developing country offers in the Uruguay Round and consistently plays down those of the developing countries, specifically those of the United States. In addition, he definitely overstates the unanimity of developing countries and Latin America on some issues.

There are some factual errors in Abugattas's chapter, but I won't go into all of them because I'm not an expert on the Round. I would just like to touch on a few because they do affect offers made by the US government. In the tariff negotiations, the US offer to cut tariffs 40 percent on a global basis goes far beyond the mandate of Punta del Este, and certainly beyond Montreal's mandate of 30 percent. In fact, only a handful of countries—the United States, Canada, Australia, New Zealand, Hungary, and Czechoslovakia—made comprehensive offers at that level. Abugattas's tropical product section estimated, incorrectly, the marginal tariff reductions implied by the offers and ignored the fact that 75 percent of US imports of tropical products come in duty free either under the Most Favored Nation Clause or the Generalized System of Preferences. Abugattas confuses our Montreal offer on tropical products with our current offer, which, according to the GATT secretariat, is by far the most ambitious offer to date in terms of trade liberalization. Abugattas also fails to note that trade among developing countries in tropical products is, while perhaps not a decisive factor, increasingly important. According to the United Nations Conference on Trade and Development and the Economic Commission for Latin America, the participation of the developing nations in liberalizing the trade in tropical products, which by rights should be important, was evident in the offers made in the Uruguay Round.

On trade-related aspects of intellectual property rights, Abugattas implies more effect than the new disciplines could create. They may cause some development difficulties for the developing countries, but I have not received empirical data to support this. In some narrow areas, countries that have adopted intellectual property protection have discovered that they flourish with it. For example, after a long process of negotiation, Italy adopted intellectual property protection in pharmaceuticals. That industry is now booming and consequently finds it easier to attract research and development money. Japan and Korea—also after considerable opposition—did the same and found the results to be less terrifying and far more profitable than they had originally expected.

Whatever its drawbacks, Abugattas's chapter has great merit because it points out the tremendous differences that exist when different parties, inside the same system, attempt to interpret the same documents. They can, and do, emerge with radically dissimilar concepts about what should be negotiated.

# Conclusion: The New
# Latin American Trade Opportunities

*Carolyn Lamm*

To varying extents, all of the ongoing changes in international economic relations (e.g., the Uruguay Round, EC '92, changes in Eastern Europe, and the US-Mexico free trade agreement) will have an impact on Latin America. The international trade climate is changing so drastically that economic alliances may supplant military agreements in future assessments of "national security."

It is critical that Latin America not allow current opportunities to pass: the general goal of the initiatives now under way is to abolish barriers to trade. In order to take full advantage of the new order, however, the Latin American nations must make their opinions known. They must actively participate, not only in the Enterprise for the Americas Initiative (EAI) and the Uruguay Round but also—to the greatest extent possible— in the regulatory process of the European Community (EC). In this way, Latin America may ensure fair treatment of its exports and create avenues for the flow of capital into its collective economy. Agreements are being reached that will change the face of international trade, and Latin America must ensure its inclusion.

Reaching any multilateral agreement will certainly require concessions. Agreement, however, requires concessions from both parties and generally benefits all concerned. For example, Brazil may find it difficult to agree to concessions regarding intellectual property protection. Foreign investors, however, are reluctant to enter joint ventures in Brazil without intellectual property security. The terms of agreement may require little more than a minor conveyance of statutory protection for intellectual property, but that concession will serve to lower a threshold and allow increased flow of capital, thereby benefiting both Brazilian and US joint venture partners.

At the same time, it is very important that the views of the industrial sector be given strong consideration during the final negotiations in the Uruguay Round. Although there can be little doubt that the United States will be Latin America's closest trading partner through the 1990s, the importance of the Uruguay Round to Latin America's worldwide trade cannot be overemphasized.

While the Uruguay Round would level the worldwide playing field, EC '92 will in effect create the world's largest single market. What that entity will look like is still uncertain. Only a portion of the nearly three hundred individual directives necessary to effect the economic union have been adopted at the community level, and they still require ratification at the national level. At both the community and national level, diplomatic efforts will be important elements of success. It is each country's responsibility to make itself heard. Latin America now has the opportunity to participate in the formation of a new and potentially very lucrative market, and it would be well-advised to make that market as receptive to Latin America's needs as possible.

It is in Latin America's interest to ensure it is not foreclosed from the EC by adverse regulations, primarily because the single market will very likely allow deeper import penetration. One study has shown that some of the most favorable conditions will be created for those commodities of which Latin America is a major exporter.

Furthermore, it has become apparent that Latin America will not be ignored by the EC. The December 1990 signing of the Act of Rome by the EC and the eleven-member "Group of Rio" is a clear indication of intent on the part of the EC to institutionalize dialogue and foster economic relations. The extent to which such an agreement will be implemented is uncertain, but it is clear that Latin America can benefit from EC '92 if it coordinates efforts to ensure it is not excluded.

Much emphasis has been placed on the possible diversion of capital from Latin America to Eastern Europe. Although a new challenge, Latin American industries hold strong competitive advantages over their Eastern European counterparts. While Latin American infrastructure may be crumbling in places, Eastern Europe's infrastructure is all but nonexistent. The Latin American region also possesses abundant natural resources, and while it does have notable environmental problems, they are reversible and not nearly as pervasive as those in Eastern Europe. Latin American countries will generally be exempted from time-consuming reviews and even denial of permission that are standard in the transfer of high technology equipment to former Warsaw Pact members. Most importantly, most Latin American nations share a legacy of market economics: managers and workers understand the importance of quality and efficiency in manufacturing a competitive stance; the workers and managers of Eastern Europe's command economies will have to learn the basic principles of market economics before they can hope to compete. As long as Latin America takes the initiative, its nations should enjoy a good deal of foreign investment.

The programs that hold the most promise, however, are the regional initiatives sponsored by the United States. While the Caribbean Basin Initiative and the Andean Countries Initiative have brought about fairly significant progress in trade, the Brady Plan and the EAI promise to attack Latin America's economic difficulties at their roots, setting the stage for a free trade area that potentially could be as significant and as internationally influential as the EC. Through programs of aggressive debt reduction—including the "debt-for-nature" exchanges based on an understanding that South America possesses ecological resources of global importance—Latin American debt can be brought under control, allaying the fears of potential investors. With restored investor confidence, debt burdens will erode under a wave of new capital.

Ultimately, it is hoped that the EAI will result in a hemispheric free trade agreement like that under negotiation between Mexico, Canada, and the United States. The effects on each country of a hemispheric trade agreement would be largely a factor of its degree of involvement in the negotiating process.

Involvement is the single most important guideline to keep in mind through future efforts. Regardless of the negotiating forum, it is critical that each country make its concerns known. The best negotiations in the world are worthless if their goals are misdirected. Careful attention to, and analysis of, the advantages and disadvantages attached to each new international initiative must not be overlooked. Most importantly, the countries of Latin America must be willing to take on the difficult internal decisions necessary to implement internal programs that will produce economic stability. That, coupled with new found political order, will encourage foreign investment and future economic growth.

# Bibliography

*Marian Goslinga*

Aguilar Zinser et al. "A Mexican Agenda." *Hemisphere* 3, no. 2 (Winter/ Spring 1991): 21.

Aragäo, José María. "INTAL: objetivos, actividades, evolución y contribución al proceso de integración latinoamericana en el período 1965-1975." *Integración Latinoamericana* 15, no. 159 (August 1990): 23-35.

Barbosa, Rubens Antonio. "Diez años de ALADI: lecciones y perspectivas." *Integración Latinoamericana* 15, no. 160 (September 1990): 24-28.

Basdeo, S. "The Single European Act: A CARICOM Perspective." *Journal of Interamerican Studies and World Affairs* 32 (Summer 1990): 103-20.

Bonnet, Roberto Junguito. "Relaciones entre la Comunidad Económica Europea y el Grupo Andino." *Integración Latinoamericana* 15, no. 161-62 (October/November 1990): 33-37.

Bose, Mihir. "Free Trade, Canada and the European Challenge." *Accountancy* (United Kingdom) 106, no. 1166 (October 1990): 101-2. Compares the US-Canada Free-Trade Agreement with the European Common Market.

Bundy, Kelly. "Advancing the Goal of a Free Trade Hemisphere." *Global Trade* 110, no. 11 (November 1990): 32-34. Discusses the pending US-Mexico agreement as well as the Enterprise for the Americas Initiative.

155

"Caribbean Basin Initiative [Revisions]." *Congressional Quarterly Weekly Report* 48 (August 18, 1990): 2687-89. A good source of information for treaties/agreements involving the United States.

"CBI, Other Matters in Conference [Customs and Trade Act of 1990]." *Congressional Quarterly Weekly Report* 48 (May 19, 1990): 1541.

Chandra, Satish. "An Examination of the Free Trade Agreement between the United States and Canada." *Tennessee's Business* 1 (Spring 1990): 15-19.

Committee for Development Planning. *Regional Trading Blocs: A Threat to the Multilateral Trading System?* New York: United Nations, 1990. UN publication ST/ESA/219.

Crookell, Harold. *Canadian-American Trade and Investment under the Free Trade Agreement.* Quorum Books, 1990.

de Clercq, Willy. "The United States and the European Community: Brothers yet Foes?" *European Affairs* 3 (Autumn 1987): 16-24.

Deere, Carmen Diana. "A CBI Report Card." *Hemisphere* 3, no. 1 (Fall 1990): 29-31.

del Bosco, Guillermo. "Propuesta institucional para la Cuenca del Plata." *Integración Latinoamericana* 15, no. 161-62 (October/November 1990): 72-74. About integration in the Southern Cone.

Elving, R. D. "Finance Panel Backs Extension of Caribbean Import Rules." *Congressional Quarterly Weekly Report* 48 (March 3, 1990): 649.

———. "Senate Backs Caribbean Bill, Declines to Broaden Scope." *Congressional Quarterly Weekly Report* 48 (April 28, 1990): 1248-50.

"Framework Trade Accord Strengthens Mexico's Role as 'US Intermediary.'" *Mexico and Central America Report* (February 21, 1991).

Fritsch, Winston. "Domestic Trade Reform and Policies towards the Trade System: Is There a Common Latin American Agenda?" Prepared for the Working Group on Economics of the Inter-American Dialogue, May 1990.

Fuentes Hernández, Alfredo, and María Clara Rueda. "Europa y América Latina: relaciones entre bloques comerciales en el decenio de 1990." *Integración Latinoamericana* 15, no. 161-62 (October/November

1990): 3-20. Analysis of trade flows between the European Community and the *Asociación Latinoamericana de Integración*.

Garrido, Germán. "Space-Age Business Consulting." *Hemisphere* 3, no. 2 (Winter/Spring 1991): 32-33.

Georgiu, George C., and Francisco E. Thoumi. "Corrientes comerciales entre Estados Unidos y América Latina: 1967-1985." *Integración Latinoamericana* 144 (Buenos Aires, April 1989): 23-30.

Gill, Henry S. "Economic Implications for Latin America and the Caribbean of Changes in Eastern Europe." Paper presented at the Conference on the Crisis in Eastern Europe: The Emerging New World Order and Its Implications for the Third World, Institute of International Relations, The University of the West Indies, St. Augustine, May 1990.

Globerman, S. "Trade Liberalization and Competitive Behavior: A Note Assessing the Evidence and the Public Policy Implications." *Journal of Policy Analysis and Management* 9 (Winter 1990): 157-89. About the US-Canada Free Trade Agreement.

Gonzalez, Anthony P. "The View from the Caribbean." *Hemisphere* 3, no. 1 (Fall 1990): 26-28.

Grabendorff, Wolf. "European Community Relations with Latin America: Policy without Illusions." *Journal of Interamerican Studies and World Affairs* 4 (1987-88): 69-87.

Graham, Bob. "Trade-offs? The US and the Caribbean." *Hemisphere* 3, no. 1 (Fall 1990): 2-3.

Griffith, Winston H. "CARICOM Countries and Appropriate Technology." *World Development* 18 (June 1990): 845-58.

———. "CARICOM Countries and the Caribbean Basin Initiative." *Latin American Perspectives* 17 (Winter 1990): 33-54.

Grinspun, Ricardo. "Free-Trade Lessons from Canada." *Hemisphere* 3, no. 2 (Winter/Spring 1991): 26-31.

Halperín, Marcelo. "La armonización de políticas económicas en el futuro de ALADI." *Integración Latinoamericana* 15, no. 160 (September 1990): 49-57.

Hollerman, Leon. *Japan's Economic Strategy in Brazil: Challenge for the United States*. Lexington Books, 1988.

Hurtado, Osvaldo. "Aspectos políticos de la integración latinoamericana." *Integración Latinoamericana* 15, no. 153 (January/February 1990): 3-8.

Institute of International Finance. *Fostering Foreign Direct Investment in Latin America.* Washington, DC: Institute of International Finance. July 1990.

Inter-American Development Bank, Institute for Latin American Integration. *El proceso de integración en América Latina.* Buenos Aires: BID/INTAL. Annual publication.

Izcúe, Joaquín. "La cooperación técnica internacional para el comercio exterior en América Latina y el Caribe." *Integración Latinoamericana* 15, no. 157 (June 1990): 19-34. Describes the activities and programs of international and/or regional agencies in the area.

Khazeh, K., and D. P. Clark. "A Case Study of Effects of Developing Country Integration on Trade Flows: The Andean Pact." *Journal of Latin American Studies* 22 (May 1990): 317-30.

Krause, L. "Trade Policy in the 1990's: Good-bye Bipolarity, Hello Regions." *World Today* 46 (May 1990): 83-84. Emphasizes the importance of regional blocs in world trade.

Lagos, Gustavo. "La creación del Instituto para la Integración de América Latina (INTAL)." *Integración Latinoamericana* 15, no. 159 (August 1990): 5-8. The author has been director of INTAL since its creation in 1969.

Macchiarola, F. J. "Mexico as a Trading Partner." *Proceedings of the Academy of Political Science* 37, no. 4 (1990): 90-109. Background article to the current negotiations.

Magariños, Gustavo. "Primer decenio de la ALADI: principios e instituciones." *Integración Latinoamericana* 15, no. 160 (September 1990): 10-23.

Marshall, Patrick G. "North-America Trade Pact: A Good Idea? The U.S.-Canada Free-Trade Pact, Which Took Effect Early This Year, May Serve as a Model for Future Bilateral Pacts with Mexico, the Caribbean and Central America." *Editorial Research Reports* (publishing arm of the *Congressional Quarterly* in Washington, DC), December 8, 1989: 682-95.

McCann, J. E., and L. Gómez-Mejía. "Exploring the Dimensions of an International Social Issues Climate." *Human Relations* 43 (Fall 1990): 141-67. About the Caribbean Basin Initiative.

McClenahan, John S. "Road to Mexico Will Be Long." *Industry Week* 239, no. 14 (July 16, 1990): 74. Discusses the difficulties to be surmounted before a trade agreement can be signed.

McCulloch, R. "The United States-Canada Free Trade Agreement." *Proceedings of the Academy of Political Science* 37, no. 4 (1990): 78-80.

"Mexico—Key Player in Regional Trade Bloc." *Central America Report* XVIII, no. 2 (January 18, 1991).

Miller, Morris. "El acuerdo de libre comercio entre Canadá y Estados Unidos: lecciones para América Latina." *Integración Latinoamericana* 15, no. 153 (January/ February 1990): 24-34. This monthly periodical, published by the *Instituto para la Integración de América Latina* in Buenos Aires, is an excellent source of information on the process of integration in Latin America. In addition to scholarly articles, it regularly features data on regional agencies and events of topical interest.

Mohn, Ingrid. "U.S.-Mexico Free Trade Agreement Means Greater Mutual Prosperity: Frequently Asked Questions about the Free Trade Agreement." *Business America* 111, no. 19 (October 6, 1990): 3-6.

Moneta, Carlos Juan. "Relaciones comerciales y financieras de América Latina con Japón y Estados Unidos: el papel del comercio, la asistencia y los flujos financieros." *Integración Latinoamericana* 144 (Buenos Aires, April 1989): 11-22.

Nau, Henry R. "Domestic Trade Politics and the Uruguay Round: An Overview." In *Domestic Trade Politics and the Uruguay Round*, edited by Henry R. Nau. New York: Columbia University Press, 1989.

Nau, Henry R. *The Myth of America's Decline: Leading the World Economy into the 1990s*. New York: Oxford University Press, 1990.

Nau, Henry R. "The NICS in a New Trade Round." In *Hard Bargaining Ahead: U.S. Trade Policy and Developing Countries*, edited by Ernest H. Preeg. New Brunswick, N.J.: Transaction Books, 1985.

"A New Retail Frontier? Last Year's Free Trade Agreement with Canada May Present New Opportunities Up North for American Retailers and Vendors." *Discount Merchandiser* 30 (January 1990): 27-30.

"Los países de menor desarrollo económico relativo en los programas de integración de América Latina." *UN Economic Commission for Latin America and the Caribbean*. Santiago: CEPAL, 1990.

Pazos, Felipe. "La integración como vía para reactivar la economía latinoamericana." *Integración Latinoamericana* 15, no. 153 (January/February 1990): 9-14.

Pease, Don J., and Terry L. Bruce. "Congress Responds." *Hemisphere* 3, no. 2 (Winter/Spring 1991): 19.

Pelzman, J., and G. K. Schoepfle. "The Impact of the Caribbean Basin Economic Recovery Act on Caribbean Nations' Exports and Development." *Economic Development and Cultural Change* 38 (July 1990): 845-54. Update and discussion of the original article, which was published in 36 (July 1988): 753-96.

Peña, Félix. "La integración latinoamericana en el decenio de 1990: ¿tiene aún sentido?" *Integración Latinoamericana* 15, no. 159 (August 1990): 36-40.

Portes, Alejandro. "An Informal Path to Development?" *Hemisphere* 3, no. 2 (Winter/Spring 1991): 4-5.

Puente Leyva, Jesús. "México: desafíos de la integración económica (oportunidades al Norte, compromisos al Sur)." *Integración Latinoamericana* 15, no. 161-62 (October/November 1990): 66-71.

Quijandría Salmón, Jaime. "ALADI 1980-1990: dificultades para reorientar un proceso que empezó mal." *Integración Latinoamericana* 15, no. 160 (September 1990): 29-37.

Raby, Jean. "The Investment Provisions of the Canada-United States Free Trade Agreement: A Canadian Perspective." *American Journal of International Law* 84 (April 1990): 394-443. The author argues that the terms are favorable to Canadian interests.

Riche, Nancy. "Canadian Labor Speaks Out." *Hemisphere* 3, no. 2 (Winter/Spring 1991): 27+.

Robinson, Randy. "Colonizing Canada: A Year and a Half of Free Trade." *Multinational Monitor* 11 (May 1990): 10-13.

Rochlin, James. "The Evolution of Canada as an Actor in Inter-American Affairs." *Millennium* 19 (Summer 1990): 229-48.

Rosenblatt, Julius, et al. *The Common Agricultural Policy of the European Community, Principles and Consequences.* Washington, DC: International Monetary Fund. November 1988.

Rugman, Alan M. *Multinationals and Canada-United States Free Trade.* University of South Carolina Press, 1990.

Sanderson, Steven E. "Free Trade: Can Mexico Win?" *Hemisphere* 3, no. 2 (Winter/Spring 1991): 16-24.

Sassen, Saskia. "Free Trade and Immigration." *Hemisphere* 3, no. 2 (Winter/Spring 1991): 2-3.

Schott, Jeffrey. "The Mexican Free-Trade Illusion: A U.S.-Mexico Trade Agreement Does Not Presage a Unified Market like the EC—And It May Not Even Lead to Free Trade." *International Economy* 4 (June-July 1990): 32-34.

"SELA: sector de servicios en las negociaciones multilaterales." *Integración Latinoamericana* 14, no. 151 (November 1989): 45-46.

Stallings, Barbara. "The Reluctant Giant: Japan and the Latin American Debt Crisis." *Journal of Latin American Studies* 22 (February 1990).

Sutton, Paul. "1992: The EC and the Caribbean." *Hemisphere* 3, no. 1 (Fall 1990): 24-25.

Taylor, Alan R. "U.S.-Canada Free Trade Success Gives Impetus to Mexico Talks." *Financier* 14, no. 7 (July 1990): 26-28.

US International Trade Commission. *The Likely Impact on the United States of a Free Trade Agreement with Mexico.* Washington, DC: US International Trade Commission. February 1991.

US International Trade Commission. *Review of Trade and Investment Liberalization Measures by Mexico and Prospects for Future United States Mexican Relations: Phase II: Summary of Views on Prospects for Future United States Mexican Relations.* Washington, DC: US International Trade Commission. October 1990.

van Klaveren, Alberto. "European-Latin American Relations in a World in Flux: From Optimism to Fatalism to Realism." Prepared for a workshop of the Inter-American Dialogue, Airlie House, May 1990.

Wade, John. "Taking the Initiative: The 'Enterprise for the Americas' Proposal." *Business Venezuela* (September/October 1990): 14-15. Comments on Latin American reactions to President Bush's June 1990 proposal.

Weitz, Mario Alejandro. "La experiencia de Europa 1992 y su influencia en América Latina." *Integración Latinoamericana* 15, no. 155 (April 1990): 31-43. Considering the success of the European Community, the author urges the speedy economic integration of Latin America.

Whaley, John, ed. *Rules, Power and Credibility*. Vol. I, *Thematic Studies from a Ford Foundation Project on Developing Countries and the Global Trading System*. London, Ontario: Centre for the Study of International Economic Relations, The University of Western Ontario, 1988.

"White House Fact Sheet on the 'Enterprise for the Americas Initiative Act' of 1990, September 14, 1990." *Weekly Compilation of Presidential Documents* (United States) 26 (September 17, 1990): 1372-76.

Whittingham, Wilfred. "The United States Government's Caribbean Basin Initiative." *CEPAL Review* (December 1989): 73-92. Reviews the CBI's achievements in the light of the objectives and expectations.

Wiemann, Jürgen. *The Implications of the Uruguay Round and the Single Market for the European Community's Trade Policy towards Developing Countries*. Berlin: German Development Institute, 1990.

# Contributors

**Luis Abugattas** is a specialist in international trade issues and a leading Latin American analyst on the General Agreement on Tariffs and Trade (GATT). His work focuses on the development of research and position papers on the Uruguay Round of GATT. He is also an adviser to a number of Andean governments on trade issues.

**Myles Frechette**, a career diplomat with the US Department of State, was appointed assistant US trade representative for Latin America, the Caribbean, and Africa in August 1990. He is responsible for the implementation of the trade pillar of the Enterprise for the Americas Initiative. Ambassador Frechette speaks Portuguese, Spanish, and French. Most of his assignments have been in Latin America.

**Marian Goslinga** is the Latin American and Caribbean librarian at Florida International University.

**Wolf Grabendorff** is director of the *Instituto de Relaciones Europeo-Latinoamericanas* (IRELA) in Spain. His research has focused on Latin American foreign policy, security affairs, and political development. He is co-author of *Lateinamerika - wohin?* and *Brasilien: Entwicklungsmodell und Aussenpolitik*, and co-editor of *Political Change in Central America: Internal and External Dimensions* and *Latin America, Western Europe and the United States: Reevaluating the Atlantic Triangle.*

**Gary C. Hufbauer** is the Marcus Wallenberg Professor of international financial diplomacy in the School of Foreign Service and Department of Economics at Georgetown University and Senior Fellow at the Institute for International Economics. From 1977 to 1980, he served as deputy assistant secretary in the US Treasury, where he was responsible for trade policy during the Tokyo Round. Dr. Hufbauer has published extensively on international trade, finance, and tax policy, and frequently testifies before the US Congress on trade-related issues. He is a member of the bar in the District of Columbia and in Maryland.

**Tetsuro Iino** is a research associate for Latin America and the Caribbean at the Carter Center in Atlanta, Georgia. For the previous twenty-five years, he was employed by one of Japan's leading trade companies, C. Itoh & Co., Ltd., a globally integrated conglomerate involved in import-export, joint-venture, and investment transactions. At C. Itoh, he served as director of North American affairs in its Overseas Planning and Coordinating Department, and as manager in charge of importing Brazilian iron ore and exploring for new iron ore deposits.

**Carolyn Lamm** is a partner with the international law firm of White & Case, at its Washington office. She is primarily involved in the representation of foreign corporate clients and foreign governments on trade and arbitration matters. Her bar memberships include the US Court on International Law. In addition, Ms. Lamm serves on the Board of Editors for *International Business Review* and is a member of the Secretary of State's Advisory Committee on Private International Law.

**Henry Nau** is the associate dean of the Elliot School of International Affairs and professor of political science at George Washington University. He served as a senior staff member of the National Security Council from 1981 to 1983, where he directed the Division for International Economic Affairs (including East-West trade). His recent books include *The Myth of America's Decline: Leading the World Economy in the 1990s* and *Domestic Trade Politics and the Uruguay Round*. Dr. Nau is a member of the Council on Foreign Relations.

**Riordan Roett** is the Sarita and Don Johnston Professor of political science and director of the Latin American Studies Program at The Johns Hopkins University School of Advanced International Studies in Washington, DC. He is the author of numerous books, including *Paraguay: The Legacy of Personalist Politics* and *Latin America, Western Europe and the US: Reevaluating the Atlantic Triangle*. Dr. Roett is co-publisher of the quarterly report, "Latin American Economic Outlook: Argentina, Brazil and Mexico." He is a member of the Council on Foreign Relations and a consultant to the World Economic Forum in Geneva, Switzerland.

**Mark B. Rosenberg** is a professor of political science and director of the Latin American and Caribbean Center at Florida International University. He has published numerous scholarly works, including three books on Central American affairs. Dr. Rosenberg is a permanent consultant to the US Institute of Peace on Latin America and the Caribbean, a vice-chair of the International Economic Development Committee of the Greater Miami Chamber of Commerce, and a member of the Executive Committee of the World Trade Center of South Florida.

**Jeffrey J. Schott** is a Research Fellow at the Institute for International Economics. From 1974 to 1982, he was an international economist at the US Treasury. During his government tenure, he had firsthand experience in trade negotiations as a member of the US team that negotiated the Subsidies Code of the General Agreement on Tariffs and Trade during the Tokyo Round. He is the author or co-author of several recent books on trade, including *Free Trade Areas and U.S. Trade Policy*, *The Canada-United States Free Trade Agreement: The Global Impact*, and *Auction Quotas and United States Trade Policy*.

**Barbara Stallings** is associate dean (social science) of the Graduate School and professor of political science at the University of Wisconsin. She is a leading specialist on Japanese-Latin American affairs. Her most recent books are *The Reluctant Giant: Japan and the Latin American Debt Crisis* and *Banker to the Third World: US Portfolio Investment in Latin America, 1900-1986*. Widely recognized for her academic leadership, she serves on the editorial boards of numerous publications.